An Illuminated Guide to Wicca

A Complete Visual Manual

Written and Illustrated by
HELENA DOMENIC

REDFeather™
MIND | BODY | SPIRIT

An Imprint of Schiffer Publishing, Ltd.

"Red Feather Mind Body Spirit Feather" logo is a registered trademark of Schiffer Publishing, Ltd.

Cover design by Ashley Millhouse
Type set in John Mayer/Minion

ISBN: 978-0-7643-6280-4
Printed in India

Published by REDFeather Mind, Body, Spirit
An imprint of Schiffer Publishing, Ltd.
4880 Lower Valley Road
Atglen, PA 19310
Phone: (610) 593-1777; Fax: (610) 593-2002
Email: Info@redfeathermbs.com
Web: www.redfeathermbs.com

For our complete selection of fine books on this and related subjects, please visit our website at www.redfeathermbs.com. You may also write for a free catalog.

Not Christian or Jew or Muslim, not Hindu, Buddhist, Sufi, or Zen.

Not any religion or cultural system. I am not from the East or the West, not out of the ocean or up from the ground, not natural or ethereal, not composed of elements at all.

I do not exist, am not an entity in this world or the next, did not descend from Adam and Eve or any origin story.

My place is the placeless, a trace of the traceless. Neither body nor soul.

I belong to the beloved, have seen the two worlds as one and that one call to and know, first, last, outer, inner, only that breath-breathing human being.

~ jelaluddin rumi

ACKNOWLEDGMENTS

Insert drop cap "A" as first word, using author's illustration for letter "A" book like this could not exist without the assistance and love of many people. I wish first to acknowledge the assistance and love of my husband, Sean Wills. Sean has supported and stood beside me through the many trials, tribulations, errors, and successes of my life, both magical and mundane. Sometimes his support has been as practical as cleaning the house and doing the laundry, and other times it has been much deeper—a shoulder to cry on and ears to hear, arms to hold, and a heart to love. Sean, you are my North Star and my most trusted friend, lover, husband. Words alone can not convey my thanks. You are in my heart.

This book is dedicated to the many beautiful Wiccans, witches, neopagans, heathens, Asatruar, and magickal people who helped me find my way on this path. I especially wish to dedicate this book to the memories of three sisters of the Path who all entered the Summerland during different phases of writing this book: Fran Toscani, Karen McFadden, and Peggy LaVasseur. I particularly wish to thank the Assembly of the Sacred Wheel generally, and more specifically, members of the Assembly of the Sacred Wheel: Ivo Domínguez Jr., James C. Welch, Michael Smith, Jim Dickinson, Bob and Karen Bruhin, Jessica Jordan Shoemaker, and so many more for hours and days and weekends of ritual, workshops, learning, exploring, growing. There are others outside the assembly to whom I owe much: Fred DiCostanzo, Debbie Chapnick, Caroline Kenner, Monika Leigh, Paul LaPosta, and again, so many more. To my own current coven, the Brandywine Kindred, thank you for joining me on this journey and working with many of the ideas that went into this book. I also want to thank the Brandywine Kindred for serving as models for several of the illustrations

in this book, and the members of my beloved Wolf Pack. You know who you are. I wish to share a special thank-you to my life coach Maxx Angenetta Jones for keeping me focused on the Work and this Work in particular. Thank you my Bear Sister, for always having my back.

I would also like to thank Christopher McClure at Schiffer REDFeather for talking with me and helping me to find a good project to publish, as well as my editor at Schiffer REDFeather, Peggy Kellar. Finally, but not least of all, I want to give a shout-out to Wald and Ruth Amberstone of the Tarot School and the Readers Studio for helping writers to meet publishers at their conference. This book would not have been possible without you.

To my ancestors known and unknown, I give thanks for the richness of my DNA heritage, and to my guides and spirits, I give thanks for the steadying of my shoulders, my heart, my feet in this world, and all the others.

Ashe, Amen, Blessed Be.

Helena Domenic

TABLE OF CONTENTS

FOREWORD

by Courtney Weber

icca has called you.

Now what?

The path for the new witch is exhilarating—and confusing. Surrounded by new experiences, feelings, insights, there's as much terror as wonder. Where do I start? Whom do I talk to? Whom can I trust with this new path?

You can breathe a little easier. You have discovered Helena Domenic.

As a public witch, Tarot reader, and author, Helena has been part of my world for well over a decade. I had just begun dating the man I would eventually marry. He was a member of large, strong Wiccan tradition community. Helena was a warm, grounding presence. Although she held a powerful role within the community, she was forever approachable. Wise and articulate with a precocious twinkle in her eye, she was someone I knew immediately that I could trust. She was smart and fun, carrying the aura of someone I felt I'd known for many lifetimes. I was far from the only person who felt that way about her.

I knew Helena first as a priestess, and then as a friend. She would ultimately preside at my wedding. She has always been a warm, comforting presence, and a guide. She shares knowledge deeply rooted in experience, thought, and profound insight. But one of Helena's many gifts is not only how she articulates in words, but also how she expresses the mystical in art.

We are visual creatures. We crave beauty. We love lovely things. Even as someone whose medium is the written word, I recognize the power of image. Helena has created a gift both for the seeker and the practitioner, a guide that makes the complicated accessible, a contextual companion. Helena's work is authentic. It comes from a place of great knowledge and experience, but also from a place of great love. Helena is a natural and experienced teacher and artist, and her work is deeply rooted in the desire to help, support, and transform.

I was delighted when Helena published this exceptional work. *An Illuminated Guide To Wicca* is what the pagan world needs right now. The boom of social media has certainly provided crucial outlets for those who want to experience magick, but the problem with the plethora of outlets is the plethora of misinformation. Authors such as Helena Domenic are exactly whom we need right now. Helena's book is particularly integral since it doesn't simply dictate instructions. Through her artistic prowess, she shows the would-be next steps, creating a ritual space directly on the page. Her work is clear, accessible, easy to follow. Most of all, it's beautiful. Not only will this be a helpful read, but a pleasurable one. It is one that not only will be helpful for those just beginning the path, but one they will return to for years to come.

The world has a lot to learn from Helena. She has helped innumerable students over the years, both those in traditional education and those on the esoteric path. She is a bright, gifted soul whose work will surely help transform the work of others. If you are fortunate enough to know her, as I do, you know you are blessed with the presence of a great soul. If you never have the opportunity to meet her, you are blessed to know her work.

Good luck to you on your journey and enjoy this magnificent book!

With every good wish,

WHY ANOTHER BOOK ON WICCA?

nother book about Wicca? Why, indeed. There are so many books available nowadays, from the late Scott Cunningham to Ray Buckland to the late Ellen Cannon Reed's wonderful *Heart of Wicca* to more-recent entries from Christopher Penczak and Devin Hunter. Why on earth would we need another one?

I've always maintained that if you line up ten Wiccans and ask them to give their definition of what Wicca is, you will get eleven different definitions. This book is mine. Who am I? I was a member of the Assembly of the Sacred Wheel from 1986 to 2018, a high priestess in that tradition since 1994, and an elder since 2003. Being a member of the assembly served me very long and very well, I am happy to say; however, I soon heard the call of my heart and my art and left to pursue the joys of both and determine exactly what I wanted my spirituality to look like. I know there are many independent, eclectic souls like mine out there. This book—its writings and its artwork—is for you, the reader who enjoys learning through visual representations. I am a very visual learner and have found that I remember information much better if it is encoded in a visual format. This book is illuminated, inspired by my love of eighth- and ninth-century Hiberno-Saxon manuscripts and the golden age of children's book illustration.

Additionally, one of my vocations in life is teaching—it fills my soul. I love to share what I know with others, because I get so much in return. As an artist and an educator, I have always used visual means both to learn and to teach.

There are a dazzling array of options to choose from in terms of Wiccan traditions. In the first chapter, I provide a brief (and by no means comprehensive) history of Wicca and a number of the traditions that have grown since the 1950s. Each chapter that follows builds on the previous lesson; however, there may be a few times when skipping ahead to another chapter may aid you—these prompts are included in the text. This book is by no means the absolute way to initiation—that is something that is between the initiate, his or her high priest and high priestess, and, most importantly, the gods. However, this book will be helpful to those seeking to build on their knowledge and who may wish to seek initiation in the future.

Roots and Branches on the Neo-Pagan Tree

CHAPTER ONE

A BRIEF HISTORY
OF WICCA

(with Some Forays into Neopaganism in General)

here DOES Wicca come from? Is it, as Gerald Gardner claims, a remnant of a former universal goddess religion spread across the continent of Europe? Or is that purely Gardner's invention? And who is this Gardner guy, anyway? Are all witches Wiccan? And WHY does all of this even matter? Should it matter?

What's a Gardnerian? What's an Alexandrian? Who are all these people and why do they say they are Wiccan when they are all doing such different things???

Are All Wiccans the Same?

The answer to that question is most definitely not. There are a number of Witches who wish to have no link whatsoever with Wicca, while others, who have no links to Gerald Gardner, embrace the name "Wiccan" (Who is Gardner? See below). It can be very confusing, even if you are not an outsider. Further, there are those who do not want to identify as Wiccan or witch but either want to be known under the wider term "pagan," as in non-Christian, or use more-particular terms such as "Druid" or "Astatru."

The Gardnerian Tradition

Most discussions on the history of Wicca either begin with Gerald B. Gardner or at least devote an enormous amount of time to him. There can be no doubt that he was incredibly influential in the spread of Wicca during the 1950s, whatever your opinion of him may be. Gardner is credited with spreading the use of the word "Wicca," which he asserted came from the Anglo-Saxon root word *wic*, meaning "to bend." In 1954, Gardner's book *Witchcraft Today* was published and, at the very least, introduced Wicca to mainstream culture in the United Kingdom. In *Witchcraft Today*, Gardner asserted that he had met a group of witches practicing in the New Forest of England and was initiated into their coven.

Aspersions have been cast at Gardner for a variety of reasons. He claims to have worked with a woman named Dorothy Clutterbuck, whose existence was thrown into doubt by several writers—her existence has been proved, but her involvement with a witches' coven is still uncertain (Valiente 1989). He claims that he joined the coven in 1939 but chose to wait so long to write and publish about his experiences because of England's witchcraft laws, which were not repealed until the 1950s.

Doubt has also been cast as to whether Gardner actually wrote the rituals he published in his books. He had claimed that the rituals he received from Dorothy Clutterbuck were fragmentary and needed to be fleshed out. There are other allegations that either Aleister Crowley had written the rituals for him, or at the very least, the gifted writer Doreen Valiente actually wrote the rituals. My intent here is not to support either claim, but to highlight Gardner as an early creator of a Wiccan tradition.

Gardner had been a civil servant, born in 1884, who spent most of his working life in Malaysia. He had a lifelong interest in different cultures and anthropology. He no doubt read Margaret Murray's book *The Witch-Cult in Western Europe*, which at the time caused a sensation by suggesting that all of Europe had at one time been united under a single pagan cult in ancient times.

During the late nineteenth and twentieth centuries, one could argue that a kind of neopagan revival was taking place—this could be attributed to the works of Margaret Murray, as well as the formation of the Hermetic Order of the Golden Dawn, the rise of the Rosicrucians, and an upswing in an interest in the occult. I would argue that neopagan revivals have taken place throughout history, possibly beginning in the Renaissance, with its interest in reviving Greco-Roman art forms and ideas.

Margaret Murray was not the only scholar writing about the possibility of a prehistoric matrifocal culture throughout Europe during Gardner's time; the idea was quite popular and being explored by writers such as Johann Jakob Bachofen and Erich Neumann. Robert Grave's work *The White Goddess* was quite well known, and although it is known as an inspired text, it was taken by some to be literal truth. Today, scholars such as Marijas Gimbutas continue studies into this area, although critics argue that there is no conclusive proof that matriarchal societies ever existed.

Margaret Murray's book *The Witch Cult of Ancient Europe* also promoted the notion of a universal stag god throughout ancient Europe. The notion has been embraced by neopagans, since it has been suggested that the god of the old religion became the devil of the new religion.

Gardner is responsible for the founding of what is known as the Gardnerian tradition of witchcraft. This is a tradition that is very interested in being able to trace its lineage back to Gardner. A Gardnerian coven's high priestess will be able to recite her lineage of having been taught by her high priestess, who was taught by another high priestess, going all the way back to Gardner. Gardner's form of Wicca is known for secrecy, strict hierarchy, and ritual scourging. Gardner's original rituals seem to have much in common with Solomonic rituals. As to the claim of Aleister Crowley having written the rituals, the two men were acquainted. Gardner had been initiated into the Ordo Templi Orientis (OTO) and said that although he and Crowley were not acquainted for long, their association was good natured. I don't believe he'd have said this if he had been trying to keep a secret such as Crowley having written his rituals for him.

The Hermetic Order of the Golden Dawn

In 1888, the Hermetic Order of the Golden Dawn was founded. I mention this because Crowley himself had been a member, and because although short lived, the Golden Dawn had a lasting impact on what is now known as the Western tradition of magick. The Golden Dawn took inspiration from a variety of sources—Qabala, astrology, Theosophy, paganism (ancient), Tarot, and ritual. Crowley had been a member at one time (and most likely caused the schism that broke the group apart, which is a story for another time) before going on to join the OTO (Ordo Templi Orientis)—an existing group upon which he left his

own stamp. It is most likely that it is from his connection to the OTO that Gardner added material to the existing rituals he may or may not have been given.

The 1734 Tradition of Witchcraft

Robert Cochrane is another important name to know in the history of Wicca. Robert Cochrane is responsible for what is known as the 1734 tradition of Wicca, which was also known as the Clan of Tubal Cain or "the Royal Windsor Cuveen." The term "1734" is a reference to the numbers that add up to create the name YHVH, which he stated was the witch's way of saying god. Cochrane's group was small but was, and remains, influential. Sadly, Cochrane died of a drug overdose in 1966, and a man named Ronald White took over leadership of the group. They are quite secretive and were nearly unknown for a very long time. Thanks to Ronald Hutton's book *The Triumph of the Moon* (Hutton 1999), there seems to be a resurgence of interest in them.

The Alexandrian Tradition

Alex Sanders is the founder of Alexandrian Wicca, which looks remarkably like Gardnerian Wicca. Sanders was born in 1926 and most likely was a student of

Gardner's. The lore has it that he stole Gardner's Book of Shadows and modeled his own tradition on it. Sanders himself claimed that he had been initiated by his grandmother (in what sounds to me like an incredibly traumatic ritual) as a small child when he happened upon her doing a ritual. If Gardner had brought Wicca to the UK mainstream, Sanders and his wife, Maxine, absolutely popularized it. They often appeared in the UK press, Maxine looking glorious and blonde (and nude) during their rituals.

Sanders claimed to have initiated over a thousand witches and had proclaimed himself "the King of the Witches." Whatever else he may have done, he also initiated Janet and Stewart Farrar, who went on to write some of the best texts available on Wicca. The Farrars were journalists and as such wrote extensively about Wicca. Sadly, Stewart died recently, but as of this writing, Janet is still writing and touring at festivals and other pagan events.

Raymond Buckland is credited with bringing Wicca to the United States. Buckland had been an initiate in the Gardnerian tradition who moved to Long Island, New York. Buckland went on to write a number of his own books, as well as founding his own tradition, the Seax-Wicca tradition. *Buckland's Complete Book of Witchcraft*, also known fondly as "the Big Blue Book," is still often the first book many witches own, and it is a great how-to for beginners.

The Feri Tradition

During the 1940s, the Feri tradition was founded by Victor and Cora Anderson, who were joined by their "foster son," Gwydion Pendderwen. The Feri Tradition is still alive today, its tenets being carried on by people such as Thorne Coyle. Their website may be found here: http://www.feritradition.org/. Gwydion Pendderwen, who died in 1982 in a car accident, was well known for his beautiful recordings of his original songs.

The Georgian Tradition

In 1970, George Patterson founded the Georgian tradition in Bakersfield, California. This tradition borrows from both Alexandrian and Gardnerian Wicca, and follows Patterson's directive: "If it works, use it. If it doesn't, don't."

The Blue Star Tradition

The Blue Star tradition of Wicca was also founded in the 1970s in Pennsylvania by Frank Dufner. Blue Star Wicca has spread across the United States, and into

Ireland. It is an initiatory and thriving tradition.

NON-GARDNERIAN TRADITIONS

There were a few non-Gardnerian-related traditions that appeared during the 1970s—many of them are more neopagan than Wiccan. Some of these said that their roots, like the Gardnerian's, were ancient, while others were interested in combining the best of a variety of traditions. In 1970, Paul Huson published *Mastering Witchcraft*, which was based on traditional British witchcraft and was a do-it-yourself manual. In 1971, Lady Sheba (like Sanders, she gave herself a title: "Queen of the American Witches") claimed that her Book of Shadows was based on Gardner's.

Dianic Wicca

Out of the feminist movement came Dianic Wicca, a form of Wicca that is exclusive to women. Mention of the Horned God is not made, and the hierarchy established by Gardner is irrelevant. Most Dianic Wiccans feel that women were natural witches. Dianic Witches can work in solitary or in groups. The idea of self-initiation becomes important here, contrasting with the earlier belief that only a witch could initiate another witch, and with the Gardnerians, who believed that only a member of the opposite sex could initiate another. A more politically, socially, and ecological consciousness had begun to emerge in Wicca with Dianic Wicca. Z Budapest founded Dianic Wicca and remains active to this day; however, her attitudes toward transwomen have made her a controversial figure. Morgan McFarland created a Dianic tradition in which men could also

take part, although the main focus remains on the goddess, and no male deities.

Circle Sanctuary

Circle Sanctuary was founded in 1974 by Selena Fox and is a 501(c)(3) nonprofit Nature Spirituality church and 200-acre nature preserve. Selena Fox has also been a great advocate for Wiccans and pagans in her work through her

Lady Liberty League, advocating religious freedom and civil rights as well as serving pagan military groups through her military ministry. Circle Sanctuary is located in southwestern Wisconsin; however, Selena herself can often be found visiting pagan events across the US (http://circlesanctuary.org).

Reclaiming

In 1978, the Reclaiming Collective formed in San Francisco, which went on to become the Reclaiming Tradition. Reclaiming is arguably most famous for one of its visionaries, the writer Starhawk, who wrote *The Spiral Dance* in 1979. Reclaiming is somewhat uncommon in that it has no hierarchical structure, makes all decisions  via consensus, and was and has always been very vocal and open in political activism. By 1997, Reclaiming groups had emerged all over the world, the collective was dissolved, and it became a tradition (http://www.reclaiming.org/about/origins/history-vibra.html).

The Assembly of the Sacred Wheel

The Assembly of the Sacred Wheel had somewhat humble beginnings in 1983, when Ivo Domínguez Jr. and Jim Welch posted a flyer at their store Hen's Teeth in Wilmington, Delaware, to form a study group. That study group eventually flowered into a coven from which many other covens sprang, making the assembly one of the largest Wiccan organizations on the East Coast. Covens in the Assembly of the Sacred Wheel can currently be found in Delaware, Pennsylvania, Maryland, New Jersey, and the District of Columbia (http://sacredwheel.org).

The Black Forest Tradition

The Black Forest Circle tradition was created in 1993 by author Silver Ravenwolf in Pennsylvania. Silver is famous for publishing numerous books on Wicca and Pennsylvania hex craft. The Black Forest Circle is also an initiatory tradition and ordains eligible members to become clergy in the state of Pennsylvania (https://silverravenwolf.wordpress.com/).

Stone Circle Tradition of Wicca

The Stone Circle Tradition of Wicca (USA), as stated on their website, "is a Wiccan Mystery Tradition, which exists to promote the spiritual development of Dedicants and Initiates; to encourage responsible fulfillment of diverse Wiccan vocations (to priestxhood, priestesshood, and priesthood); and to offer service to our communities, to all in Earth's Household, and to the Divine Spirit of the Universe, One and Many, Male, Female, Both, and Neither. We recognize our responsibility to the unfolding future of Wicca as a religion." They have members in Maryland, Pennsylvania, West Virginia and Oregon (https://stonecircletraditionofwicca.wildapricot.org/Charter).

Non–Wiccan Pagan Groups

Other groups that sprang up during the 1960s and '70s in the United States include the Church of the Eternal Source, which was a group devoted to the Egyptian mysteries, and Feraferia (still in existence: http://www.phaedrus.dds.nl/fmenu.htm), which was devoted to the Greek pantheon. The Church of All Worlds (CAW) was founded in 1962 (http://www.caw.org), having evolved out of the gathering of a group of friends who were fans of Robert Heinlein's book *Stranger in a Strange Land*. CAW was officially recognized as a church in 1970 and became famous for publishing the neopagan periodical *Green Egg*.

The New Reformed Orthodox Order of the Golden Dawn (NROOGD) actually has nothing to do with the late-nineteenth-century group of a similar name and was formed in 1967 in San Francisco, California. The group evolved out of a group of students taking a class at a university in which they had an assignment to perform ritual. They began doing so and discovered that they "felt" something, liked it, and began to study and form more formally as a group. The tradition continues to this day, and although more eclectic, member covens trace their lineage back to the original group.

The Radical Faeries

In 1979, the Radical Faeries were formed by Harry Hay, a gay activist with a long history of fighting for queer rights. He and his partner, John Burnside, chose the word "faerie" to describe themselves and their movement as a taking back of that term in celebration, rather than denigration, of queerness and queer spirituality. Today, groups of Radical Faeries can be found across the United States, Canada, and the world (http://www.radfae.org/). I have found that the Radical Faeries differ greatly from region to region—some are more active politically, with not much emphasis on spirituality, while others do ritual and consider themselves a spiritual as well as political group.

Ár nDraíocht Féin

Ár nDraíocht Féin (also known as ADF) was founded by Isaac Bonewits during his college years as a joke; it was a means for him and his friends to join together on campus on Sundays to avoid church services. Ár nDraíocht Féin means "Our Own Druidism," and eventually Bonewits and other members discovered that there was something satisfying for them in Druidry. In 1983, Ár nDraíocht Féin became a true fellowship, and it received tax-exempt status in 1990. Isaac himself passed away in 2010, but ADF continues on. With Ár nDraíocht Féin, the goal is to promote awareness and education of all Indo-European practices, with an emphasis on the Celts (http://www.adf.org/core/).

Asatru

Asatru is a more recent development in neopaganism, although one might say it has been around much longer than Wicca and, indeed, was part of an older tradition that never really died out (in which case, I might say that it is in fact more recently popular). Asatru is frequently regarded as one of the neopagan family of religions. That family includes Wicca, Celtic Druidism, and re-creations of Egyptian, Greek, Roman, and other ancient pagan religions. However, many Asatruars prefer the term "heathen" to "neopagan" and look upon their tradition as "not just a branch on the Neopagan tree" but as a separate tree. Unlike Wicca, which has gradually evolved into many different traditions, the reconstruction of Asatru has been based on the surviving historical record. Its followers have maintained it as closely as possible to the original religion of the Norse people.

Asatru or Ásatrú is an Icelandic word that is a translation of the Danish word "Asetro." Asetro was first seen in 1885 in an article in the periodical *Fjallkonan*. The next recorded instance was in *Heiðinn siður á Íslandi* ("Heathen traditions in Iceland") by Ólafur Briem (Reykjavík, 1945). It means "belief in the Asir," the gods. "Asatru" is a combination of "Asa," which is the possessive case of the word Æsir (Aesir), and "Tru," which means belief or religion.

One of the more visible, active, and accessible means of working with the Asatru is through the organization known as the Troth (http://thetroth.org), which works with Asatruar and heathens internationally. Although the Asatru path has been plagued through the years by racists trying to use the northern gods for their own means, the Troth is one organization that has reliably and regularly removed such elements from their membership.

Regardless of whether one chooses to believe that Wicca is a religion that follows a path straight out of Paleolithic Europe, or is a modern creation, it certainly is a growing religion, which provides a great deal of satisfaction to its practitioners. Wicca has achieved recognition from the United States government, and although there are still many battles to be won in the area of religious tolerance, it has certainly come a long way from its initial introduction in Britain in the 1950s.

Up Next . . .

In the pages that follow, we will explore the tenets of Wicca, the Wheel of the Year followed by Wiccans, and the many things a beginning Wiccan would want to know. While this book is by no means "everything you need to know about Wicca," it is, I hope, an excellent introduction that will whet the reader's appetite for more.

CHAPTER TWO

SOME WICCAN BELIEFS

I have called this chapter "Some Wiccan Beliefs" because there are so many different beliefs that different Wiccan traditions hold dear. For each Wiccan that you speak to—and this may be even if they are in the same tradition—you will hear different beliefs. This is in part due to the fact that Wicca is very decentralized. Whether Wiccans care to admit it or not, where Wicca is now in the twenty-first century is much like where Christianity was before the fourth century CE, when the emperor Constantine decided to standardize Christian beliefs. There is no one central leader, no pope, no centralized dogma in Wicca. I believe it is both our strength and our weakness. I believe it is a strength because it allows for great individual freedom and will, I hope, keep us from being or becoming too rigid. I say it is also a weakness because it seems that wherever humans find things to divide them rather than unite them, they often go after their differences. It is a shame, because united we would have a great deal more power in the world. I am not talking about the kind of power that corrupts, but the kind that would allow us to have more say in how we are seen by the world at large, and enable us to have a visibility we have not allowed ourselves to have.

Now that I've gotten that off of my chest, allow me to talk about some of the things that seem to be common among Wiccans in our beliefs. I shall do my best to be inclusive of ALL Wiccans and try to cover a lot of ground here, explaining some of the finer points as I go. I apologize in advance for anyone or anything I may leave out or be unaware of at this writing.

The Earth Is Our Mother

If I had to choose just one belief that is central among Wiccans, it would have to be that the Earth herself is a living being, and that even if we do not agree that she is a goddess, we should at least treat her like one. When I was in graduate school pursuing my MA in art education, my thesis centered on using ritual as a pedagogical tool, and I used the neopagan community as an exemplar of ritual use. I surveyed a cross section of people from a number of different traditions about their beliefs, and the one thing everyone seemed to agree on was the divinity of the Earth.

Christians, Jews, and Muslims all believe in a heavenly paradise where they will go after death and be away from all the ills of the world. I believe such thinking has led us to where we are now—in a state of environmental chaos and climate change. Wiccans believe that the Earth is our Mother, and that we must treat her with love and respect. Deity is immanent in nature, and we honor the cycles of growth, decay, and rebirth we see in the seasons.

Honoring Both Feminine and Masculine as Divine

As you may have gathered from reading above, Wiccans do tend to honor both the female and male in the Godhead. This can take different forms among different Wiccans. On the whole, Wiccans tend to be polytheists, although there are some who believe that All Are One; however, that One contains both male and female. Others believe in many gods AND goddesses. There is also a current stream of thought that is atheist, or nontheist at least, seeing the gods and goddesses as archetypes alone.

In the tradition I was trained in, we see the gods and goddesses as beings that are bigger than humanity, who have chosen to look out for us and hear our prayers. They may robe themselves in the trimmings we provide—for example, a Mother Goddess can appear as Isis, or Demeter, or Ceres, or Frigga, depending on who is calling upon her, and for what. We can cultivate relationships with these beings, and they will help us when asked, if we maintain relationships with them.

One thing that I have observed in the time that I have been Wiccan is that definitions of male and female are changing in many ways, as well as the notion that a person can be nongender binary, and so can deity. I think that the emphasis on duality has cost Wicca some members and that we need to change as the times change. I was personally drawn to Wicca as a path because of an emphasis on a Divine Feminine, and I believe that we should not make people feel excluded by a strict adherence to duality and polarity. That is, I believe that people should be able to find their own faces in the Divine, and if that face is nongender binary, then room should be made for such.

Belief in Magick

Why do we spell magick with a "k" on the end? The reason for this goes back to Aleister Crowley. Whether you like him or not, he very helpfully said that it was necessary to make it clear that magic with a "k" is not the same as parlor tricks and sleight-of-hand exercises. Magic with a "k" is about magick that can effect change in our lives, in a myriad of ways.

Magick is often the thing that attracts people to Wicca in the first place—the notion that there is more to this world than what human eyes can see unaided. Some may find their way to Wicca because they wish to work spells; that is, they wish to change their circumstances in some way by using magick. Once people come to Wicca, they find that what they are really seeking is empowerment of themselves, which Wicca certainly provides. Having said that, magick both high and low is definitely something that Wiccans practice.

What is the difference between high and low magick? These are sometimes thrown around as value judgments, which I would prefer to stay away from—I find all magick is useful, and we need it for a variety of reasons. However, if we need to differentiate, low magick tends to be magick for one's self—attracting a lover, attracting a job, protecting one's self. High magick is the work of perfecting one's soul to become closer to the gods—to become like the gods themselves. We live in the physical world, however, and sometimes we need help on the physical plane, so I honestly do not consider any magick to be "low."

Wiccan Ethics

After the discussion above, discussing ethics is very important. If you have done any reading on Wicca at all before coming here, you have probably heard of the "Threefold Law." The Threefold Law states that whatever you send out into the universe comes back to you threefold, whether it is positive or negative. In other words, if you send out a curse on someone, it will come back on you in some shape or form. This also goes along with the statement "An' it Harm None, Do as Ye Will," which has been attributed to Gerald Gardner by way of Aleister Crowley (Crowley said, "Love is the Law, Love under Will."). Again, this idea is rather vague and open to interpretation, but essentially, do what you want but harm no one. Ethics will be covered in more depth in a later chapter.

Personal Responsibility

As you may have gleaned from the above, personal responsibility is paramount in Wicca. Counter to what popular culture (shows such as *The Chilling Adventures of Sabrina the Teenaged Witch*, the movie *The Craft*, and countless other examples) will tell us, witches do not believe in a personified evil (i.e., the devil or Satan). It is highly frustrating to have to constantly explain to people that witches are definitely not the same as Satanists, and oftimes in articles about Wicca in the mainstream media, those interviewed seem to have to spend a lot of time explaining what Wicca is not.

Because we do not believe in a centralized evil, it is entirely up to us to mind our behavior. We do believe in the laws of karma as seen in the Threefold Law; however, we also don't believe that there is something out there tempting us to do wrong and behave badly. It is entirely up to us to monitor our behavior and treat others well.

Reincarnation

Reincarnation is a core belief of Wicca. We believe that we tend to come back as humans, not as animals, and that we can choose, prior to birth, the circumstances into which we will be born to learn whatever lessons we have come here to learn. There is a notion that one day we will reunite with the Godhead, although how this takes place may vary from person to person. Some Wiccans have a more Buddhist attitude toward reincarnation—that we will continue to reincarnate until we have learned how to alleviate suffering. Reincarnation is one of those core beliefs that everyone seems to have but has differing ideas on how it plays out.

Initiation

Initiation is something that most Wiccan traditions agree on, although once again, the ways and reasons for which initiation is conferred may differ greatly from tradition to tradition. I do think most will agree that it is the gods themselves who confer initiation, and that anything humans do is merely acknowledging that it has taken place in the individual. Some traditions state that one is not truly a member of a coven until one is initiated, and then they are allowed into the inner teachings of that tradition, and others—like the tradition I was trained in—see initiation as a personal choice. The level of structure a person requires may vary from person to person, so be sure to know what is required of any group that you may wish to join.

Things You May Hear of but Are Not Universal: Going Skyclad

Skyclad is a term used to mean that one is literally "clad with the sky." That is—one is naked. I have no idea whether our witchy ancestors actually danced in the nude, or if medieval and Renaissance depictions of witches made people think that way, or if Gerald Gardner made it all up. Having said that, there are many people who love to practice their craft in this way, and you will definitely encounter lots of nudity at pagan festivals where that freedom is allowed. There are some cases in which groups are nude for all of their rituals, and some in which that is the case for coven-only rituals, and there are other groups who practice that way only for initiations. I believe this kind of thing is a personal choice and does not indicate that one way is better than another. Having said that, when you attend ritual with a new group for the first time—DO find out if this is the case, especially if you do not wish to practice in the nude.

Scourging

In Gardnerian and Alexandrian groups, scourging (meaning whipping or flogging) is a means of attaining altered consciousness and raising energy. It is certainly not everyone's cup of tea, and there are some who think Gardner included scourging in his rituals in order to satisfy a certain kink. I have no idea, again, if that is the case, and I don't have any judgment around it either. I have been told by several Gardnerians that this practice can vary greatly from group to group, both in the intensity of the scourging and the frequency. There are plenty of groups that do not scourge, so once again—I encourage you to find out ahead of time, if this is not your thing.

Sexual and Gender Attitudes

Witchcraft, Wicca, and paganism are all very open minded and welcoming to people of all sexual persuasions, and gender. This makes them very appealing to many who have not found such acceptance in their religions of family origin. I have found this attitude to be wonderful and eye opening, since when I first came to the craft, I was coming out of a very narrow-minded Roman Catholic background. Being in the craft taught me to embrace diversity. Most pagans will find people of all gender persuasions in the circles in which they travel.

These are what I have seen as the core beliefs of Wicca as I have experienced them. As I have mentioned, there is no centralized dogma, and there is a lot of room for personal experience and belief. I hope that this has given you enough room for thought, and, of course, you will make your own choices and observations as you learn.

Personal Work

Now that you have read this chapter, think about the beliefs that are important to you. Do they line up with what you have read here? What is most important to you, if you had to name one thing? Is there anything that you feel differently about? Write these thoughts down in your journal.

CHAPTER THREE

THE ELEMENTS AND RITUAL TOOLS

 hat is the most important tool in a witch's toolbox?

The answer to this question is deceptively simple and straightforward—YOU ARE. (I always tell my students, "You are the most important tool, but don't BE a tool!") You can collect all the most beautiful and fabulous wands, athames, and other tchotchkes, but if you don't put yourself into your own practice, they will mean nothing. You are the one who directs the energy; you are the one within whom the power resides. A daily practice of meditation is the key to any magickal practice. For this reason, if you are unsure about meditation and how to begin, I suggest you read chapter 9, on psychic development, to learn more about beginning a meditation practice. In the meantime, here is a discussion on the elements and the four basic tools.

There are any number of working tools that any Wiccan would need to have in his or her possession, but there are four that are absolute musts if you really want to practice Wicca both magically and in a celebratory way. These four tools are the athame, the wand, the chalice, and the pentacle. You will also need an excellent working knowledge of the elements and four directions in order to cast a circle, and really to work any kind of magic whatsoever.

What Is the Importance of a Quarters Cast Circle?

Prior to beginning ritual, most Wiccans and neopagans establish sacred space by "calling the quarters." Essentially, in doing this, we are asking for the energies of the four sacred directions to be present, as well as the elemental energies associated with them. The calls themselves vary greatly, depending on the kind of work that is to be done and the level of protection in a circle that may be needed. We'll talk about calling the quarters more in depth when discussing ritual construction.

The Pentacle and the Elements

Each element is associated with one of the four sacred directions. Some traditions handle the quarters differently and prefer different correspondences. For example, although we place Swords in the east, with Air, some prefer to place swords with Fire, and Staffs with Air. Each element is associated with a season, along with all of the other correspondences that go along with them, so that where you are standing on the planet makes a difference, as we observed with the eight sacred holidays. Some people in the United States prefer not to place Water in the west if they are on the East Coast (in this book, we will place Water in the west). In magick, procedures and approaches that have been practiced again and again over time build up power. If you are confused by which correspondences to use, pick the tradition that works best for you and **stick with it**. Over time, the associations will become stronger for you.

One way of learning how things are associated with the elements is by meditating on them and thinking of what they might remind you of. We will end this discussion with a meditation on the quarters and elements, and this will aid in your own personal understanding of them.

You may find, in your travels, that different groups use different colors to represent each quarter. As I stated above, choose whatever works for you, and stick with it. The most-common Wiccan associations with color are as follows: East is blue like the sky, or yellow like the sun; South is nearly always red—that doesn't seem to deviate; West is silver like the moon, or blue like water; and Earth is often green, but sometimes gold or yellow. In the chart included in this chapter, I have listed both the traditional colors and the tattva colors.

The tattvas are used by some Wiccans and other kinds of magicians. The tattva's are symbols that are used in Indian schools of thought, and the" word *tattva* is Sanskrit for "principle," "reality," or 'truth." The symbols are useful associations that can be used as visual place holders in meditation and ritual. In Eastern systems, the number of tattvas ranges from 25 to 36; however, for Wiccan purposes, we usually work with just five of them—one for each element, and one for spirit.

Each element is associated with an elemental ruler and elemental beings. This is more of a carryover from ceremonial magick; however, it is important to know these associations. A time may come when you may need to use them yourself, or you may be in a circle where you hear them being invoked. The elemental rulers are often referred to as the "Kings," which is of course a rather sexist term; however, these associations are very old. Each element is also associated with an archangel—again, something that comes from ceremonial magick. Some Wiccans work with the archangels, but some do not.

There are a number of ways to acquire your magical tools—they can either be bought or made by you, depending on your abilities with the various ways you might make things by hand. This author is assuming that most readers will not have access to a forge and anvil, or a potter's wheel, so, of course, one need not make their own athame or chalice by hand.

East/Athame/Air/Intellect/Spring/Dawn

Air might be cold—and sometimes hot. When someone is talking too much about themselves, we might say they are full of hot air. Most traditions associate the sword or athame with Air, although sometimes Air is associated with the wand. This author's personal preference is to associate the athame with Air and the east. In the Tarot, Air and Swords are associated with some of the harsher aspects of life. Rachel Pollack points out that when life is at its toughest, we need our minds the most—and this is where the association of Air with Swords feels appropriate to me. Swords and athames may be thought of the tools we use to cut through illusion and deception—and we all know how

Air
East
Intellect
Dawn
Sword
Sylphs
Paralda
Raphael
Yellow
to Know

painful losing our illusions can be. Air is also about cognition and, as such, is associated with the mind, the psychic, and divination.

The elemental King associated with Air is Paralda, and Raphael is the archangel. The elemental being associated with Air is the Sylph. Sylphs are creatures that might be said to be fae-like; however, their description is not what we usually think of in terms of faeries. They appear ethereal; however, they are very powerful.

The ceremonial knife used by Wiccans is typically called an "athame." We don't know exactly where this word came from. This word does not actually appear in any European language, and according to Idris Shah, who was Gerald Gardner's secretary, the word supposedly came from the Middle East and referred to the term "blood letter." Robert Graves asserted that the word came from the Arabic word for "arrow." There is nothing to really back up any of this academically, unfortunately. However, this is the word that the knife is typically known by, and it is used by all Wiccans.

The Athame is generally a double-edged blade and is typically used for casting the circle and calling the quarters. Sometimes a wand may also be used for this purpose, but an athame is believed to cast a more secure circle. The double edge is said to represent the polarity of male and female, but it can also represent the duality of light and dark, or whatever associations you may make with pairs of things.

What sort of athame should you have? There are many options out there, and more are arriving all the time as Wicca becomes more popular and more metalworkers create blades specifically for Wiccans. One option is the double-sided blade, which reflects the polarity of god and goddess. Some say the athame must have a black handle, but I believe it is truly up to the individual. I always believe in creating one's own tools when possible; however, we are not all blacksmiths, and purchasing an athame is usually what most of us do. It is important to note, however, that not all athame blades are crafted of metal. Bearing in mind that most of us will never use the athame to actually cut anything, the blade does not actually need to be functional in a traditional sense. I have seen beautiful athames crafted of wood and bone. The athame is meant to cut illusions, not steak! Additionally, if you enjoy working with the fae, it is best not to use an implement forged of or with iron, since it will drive them away.

South/Fire / Wand/Passion and Will/Summer/Noon

Fire is associated with creativity, passion, desire, and drive. It is about sexuality and pure moral drive at the same time. Fire does not like to be still, and as we can note with people who have fire signs as their sun sign, Fire likes to stir things up.

Because Fire is about the will, so the wand acts as a tool in focusing the will. Sadly, to wield our wands as they do in Harry Potter requires breaking the laws of physics; we will not be learning how to do that in this particular book. Sometimes the wand is used for casting the circle and for calling the quarters, but most often it is used to direct energy in ritual. There are some who feel that the wand has gotten "too caught up with ceremonial magick" (Buckland 1986, p. 33); however, the wand is a tool that I suspect has been used by magical practitioners of many different cultural persuasions throughout time.

The elemental king of Fire is Djinn, and the archangel is Michael. The salamanders are the elemental beings associated with Fire. It is worth noting that salamanders came to be associated with fire due to a medieval belief that they were born in fire. This is because salamanders were often found hiding under the wood in fireplaces.

What length should your wand be? I believe, once again, that this is a personal choice. There are some who will tell you that the wand must be the same length of your arm from the crook of your elbow to the tip of your middle finger. This is quite a nice guideline, actually, because it personalizes the wand to you. There are plenty of ways to personalize a wand, however.

Wand creation is much easier for most people than an athame or sword is. I don't know too many people capable of smelting their own iron, but wood is plentiful, and most people can at the very least handle sanding it. You can also

get creative in choosing the kind of wood you would wish to have for your wand—some research into wood lore would be helpful here. You can also burn designs into your wand, should it be crafted of wood, such as runes or other symbols.

Wands are made of other materials besides wood—I have seen gorgeous wands made of metal, glass, and semiprecious stones, put together through clever soldering of the materials. The kind of wand you choose for yourself really depends on what your personal preferences are, and how theatrical you might want something to be.

Both the wand and the athame are considered to be male in energy.

West/Water/Chalice/Emotion/Autumn/Dusk

Water correlates to the full range of human emotions. Water is about relationships. As Ivo Domínguez says, "Water attempts to process, to digest, and to transform whatever it touches, yet it takes the shape of any container and seeks its lowest reaches. Water responds, reacts, and is acted upon. Water is magnetic in that it seeks itself and clings to itself." (Domínguez 1996, p. 52). The ocean is often thought of as the great unconscious, and so Water also corresponds to intuition and to the Collective Unconscious.

Water's elemental king is Nixsa, and the elemental beings are Undines. The Undines are underwater beings—like and unlike mermaids. The archangel Gabriel is associated with Water.

The chalice is not mentioned by all traditions as a working tool; however, it is crucial to most Wiccan practice. The chalice is often used in ritual to share ale during the cakes-and-ale portion of ritual. The chalice also corresponds to the feminine and is used in the symbolic Great Rite, along with the athame, to represent the union of male and female.

The material of which your chalice is made depends entirely on you, and how you wish to use it in ritual. Many people like ceramic chalices with beautiful glazes, so that they can hold fluid and be used in ritual for sharing ale. I have also seen wooden chalices whose sole purpose is to hold energy, as opposed

to fluids. A chalice can also be glass, although if you are traveling with your chalice and it is made of a breakable material, I highly recommend having something safe to carry it in, such as a velvet-lined box. I have a pewter chalice that I have had since I first became Wiccan back in the 1980s, and it has served me well ever since then. My foot falls are not delicate, so I like something that is sturdy!

North/Earth/Pentacle/Stability/ Winter/Midnight

The Earth represents all that is solid, balanced, stable. It also represents the physical plane of being. Sometimes Earth gets a bad rap because it is associated with the material world (which includes money) as well. However, it is this same element of the material that makes Earth the most magical element; if we are not well grounded, if we are not stable, then it is very difficult to effectively practice magick. It is hard to see the magic in the world when we are concerned about where our next meal is coming from. It is said that the Earth is the culmination of all of the other elements—all elements exist to make up Earth. For neopagans, that makes it a magical element indeed, for an Earth-based religion.

Ghob is the elemental king of Earth, and Uriel is the archangel. The gnomes are the elemental beings of earth. They are not the adorable red, conical-hatted characters of recent depictions—they are earthy beings who work within the depths of the Earth.

The pentacle is both a symbol and a tool here. It is said that during the Burning Times, pentacles were made of wax so that they could be easily disposed of in a fire should the Christian clergy come calling. Nowadays, pentacles appear everywhere, from jewelry to door mats. The points of the pentacle itself represents the four elements plus spirit. A modern Wiccan draws an invoking pentacle in the air when invoking each element while casting a circle. The pentacle is the gate through which the element enters the circle.

A pentacle may be made of any number of materials. I have made several of my own and made several for friends by using a piece of wood and a wood

burner. There are ceramic pentacles as well as metal pentacles, each serving a purpose. A wooden pentacle may serve as a safe place to put an incense burner on an altar.

The pentacle is a symbol that has appeared from ancient to modern times. The pentacle even appears on the Ethiopian flag! The pentacle became associated with Satanism in more-recent times due to the Satanists' co-optation of a number of symbols, including the Christian cross, which they inverted.

Ether/Spirit

The top point of the pentacle represents spirit—and also acknowledges that it is present always, and the cast circle is itself also the fifth element. Still others may call Spirit into the circle separately from the four other elements once those are called. Spirit is also sometimes referred to as "Akasha." Akasha is the Sanskrit word for ether. It was Plato's Timmaeus who posited the existence of ether. Since Spirit is all around us, there is no corresponding tool to ether.

I will conclude this discussion with a brief meditation on the elements. If you can, have a friend read the meditation to you, or you can even tape yourself reading the meditation. Read slowly and leave time where indicated by the periods for pauses so that you can reflect.

Personal Work: Meditation on the Elements

Take a few moments to ground and center yourself. Breathe in, breathe out, and as you exhale, let go of any tensions you may be holding in your body. With each outward breath, feel the troubles of the day leaving you. Feel yourself rooted to the Mother Earth . . . and turn inward. Turn to that place inside you where you connect with the Divine. Know that while you are within, there is nothing that can harm you.

You are standing on a wheel, a great wheel. It is the Wheel of Time and Place. This great wheel corresponds to a great many things, but today we will focus on the directions and the elements. In your mind's eye . . . turn to the east. You are standing on a green, gently sloping hill. Before you hangs a white banner upon which a blue circle is emblazoned, the blue circle of Air. Feel calm and relaxed and notice that the sun is rising in the east. Before you, a sword lies upon the ground, its metal shimmering and reflecting the colors of the rising sun. It is a beautiful, bright morning. Flowers are in bloom all around you. The early-morning call of birdsong tells you that it is spring. The sky is an intense blue. Look around you . . . take note of all the sights and sounds. Look around to see if there are any other beings here. If there are, greet them and thank them for joining you here. Ask them if there is anything they might tell you right now that you need to know . . . listen . . . *long pause*.

The time has come to continue your journey. Thank any beings who might have come, and if it feels appropriate, leave them a gift of some sort . . .

Now turn and move to the south. The air is warmer. The sun is higher in the sky, and it is now noon. The warmth of summer has arrived. You are still standing in a beautiful, verdant field, but now you see all around more signs of life and activity. Ahead of you is another white banner, this time bearing the red triangle of Fire. There is a grove of trees just ahead, and there is what appears to be a large staff standing in the middle of the trees. Approach the staff . . . How does it appear to you? Look around to see if there are any beings here with whom you might speak . . . ask them what you need to know about Fire, and about this place. Listen carefully to any messages they may have . . . *long pause*.

The time soon comes to journey onward. Thank any beings that have come, and if it feels appropriate, leave them a gift of some sort . . .   .

You move clockwise through the field, the field that is part of the Wheel of Time. Although it is still warm, the sun has begun to set. The air grows just a little chillier. The crickets and frogs are just beginning their evening songs. Before you hangs a banner with a silver crescent on it. There are trees, but their leaves are no longer green. They are ablaze with the glorious shades of autumn. In the middle of the field, there is a well filled with crystal-clear water. Approach the well and peer in to it . . . What do you see? Does anyone approach you here in the place? If someone appears, thank them for coming and ask them what they have to tell you about this place, and . . . about Water . . . *long pause*.

The time comes for you to continue your journey on the Wheel of Time. Take a moment and thank any beings who have appeared for coming, and if you wish, you may thank them or honor them in some way . . .

You move now to the last place on the wheel. It is cold now, much colder. Because you are on the astral, the cold does not chill you, but you are aware of the change. It is midnight. A full, bright, beautiful full moon hangs over a snow-covered field. You see the banner ahead; this time it bears a yellow square. Everything is absolutely still and silent. Lying in the snow, as if waiting for your approach, is a pentacle. Take note of it. What is it made of? Is it large? Small? Heavy? Light? Reach down and pick it up. Look about to see if any beings approach you . . . if anyone comes, thank them for coming. Ask them what they might tell you about this place, and about Earth . . . *long pause*.

The time has come to complete our circuit on the Wheel of Time. But first, turn now to the center. Before you hangs, suspended in the air, the crystal-clear oval egg of Spirit. You have entered the realm of ether, the realm of pure Spirit. Look around you in this realm . . . What do you see? Look about to see if any beings approach you . . . if anyone comes, thank them for coming. Ask them what they might tell you about this place, and about Spirit . . . *long pause*. Thank any beings who have come, and if you are so moved, you may wish to thank or honor them in some way. . . . And now the time has come to turn back to the wheel itself . . . keep moving clockwise, back to the east . . . to the beginning . . . it is dawn again, the start of a new day. Take a moment and thank all of the beings and images who may have come to you at this time. Know that you can return to this place again at any time . . .

And now . . . turn back within yourself and become aware of yourself in this place and time. Feel the feeling of your feet on the floor, the feel of your clothes on your body . . . wiggle your fingers, wiggle your toes . . . remember your grounding with the Earth . . . touch the ground if needed, and return, remembering all that you have just seen.

Personal Work: Consecrating Your Tools

Once you have acquired your magickal tools, it is a good idea to consecrate them. Not all witches see this as a necessary step, so it is a personal choice. Many witches, on the other hand, see this as a way of differentiating their tools from other, everyday objects they own. This can be done very simply. In chapter 10, I describe how to cast a circle for ritual. Following the directions there, cast a circle and call the quarters. You may want to have simple markers at each quarter—you can use a compass to help you figure out where each of the directions is in your home. Once the circle is cast, bring the tool of your choice to each quarter, beginning with the east, and introduce the tool. You can do this with words you come up with on the spot, or if you wish, you may say something like this:

Powers of the East, Spirits of Air,
I bring this magical tool to you for consecration.
Bless and charge this tool with the powers of the East,
Make it sacred and special,
So Mote it Be.

You would then move to the south, the west, and the north. Once the tool has been presented to each of the quarters, give thanks to each of the quarters and dismiss the circle. If you have had any feelings or impressions while performing the ritual, write them down in your journal.

CHAPTER FOUR

GAZING MORE DEEPLY INTO THE CAULDRON

Other Important Things You Should Know

ow that we've discussed some important beginner aspects of Wicca, it is time to go deeper. Like any religion, Wicca has many facets, many tenets, and many tools and bells and whistles. Not all of the things I will be mentioning in this chapter are necessarily things that are used or observed by every Wiccan, but they are things that I have found useful and important.

Some Items You Might Want to Have

Beyond the four tools that correspond to the elements (athame, wand, chalice, pentacle), there are a number of things any well-stocked witch may want to have!

A Cauldron

A cauldron does not necessarily have to be one of those huge items that you can actually use to cook over a fire—although when you are working with a coven, it sure helps to have one! Cauldrons can be found in all shapes and sizes, and they are great for magickal and practical purposes. I have seen witches who have used cauldrons to cook up ritual soups—everyone in the coven chips in some kind of herb for the magick at hand. Most importantly, a cauldron is a

safe place to keep fires contained. Some rituals involve burning scraps of paper and the like—a cauldron is a safe place to do that. When not burning things, you can fill a cauldron with water and ink and use it to scry. Very useful!

Herb Cabinet

Not all witches become skilled herbalists; however, most do use herbs or essential oils (or both) for all kinds of magickal purposes. A time will come when you will want space

dedicated to your magickal herbs to keep them away from your kitchen herbs. The size will depend entirely on you and how much you think you need to store.

Mortar and Pestle

This item corresponds directly to the last item, because you will want to have a mortar and pestle to grind your herbs for your potions, incenses, powders, and baths. They are very easy to find in these days of places such as Whole Foods and Amazon.com. Definitely a must-have!

Incense and Incense Holder

Incense is an essential for many rituals and workings. It comes in many forms, and at some point you may want to make your own. Stick and cone incense works just fine, although you may want to make sure you are using good, well-made incense—I will have an index in the back of the book for where to purchase such items. If you are using stick incense, then the whole question of incense holders becomes much easier, since all you need is something to hold the nonburning end of the stick. For cones, you want to make sure that whatever you are burning the cone on will hold up to the heat. Finally, you can also use loose incense that you have made yourself, which can be burned on charcoals. You will definitely want something attractive and useful for this purpose, and I am including places to buy such things in the index.

Broom or Besom

The tradition I trained in did not use brooms very much, although I have used them in a very practical way to "sweep out" negative energy. The broom or besom is essentially a bundle of twigs that are bound onto a sturdier wooden pole. Now there are some stories out there about witches applying flying ointment in the Middle Ages—the flying ointment most likely had psychotropic properties, so what the broom was useful for may be left to the imagination. Nowadays, there is the sweeping away of negative energy, as previously mentioned. I have also seen witches hang a broom bristles side up on their door for protection. Additionally, I have seen the "jumping the broom" ceremony adapted for Wiccan handfastings (weddings). There are many other uses for them, and again I have listed places to find good besoms in the index.

Divination Tool(s)

I did a very unscientific study on my Facebook timeline in which I asked my Wiccan/pagan/heathen friends what their favorite magical tools were, and received a lot of responses that included Tarot cards, runes, or pendulums, or something similar. Divination is indeed important for us witches, and these tools have other applications in magic as well.

Crystals

In the same nonscientific Facebook study, many of my friends also noted that they value their crystals and rocks as magical tools. Crystals and rocks may be empowered with intentions and carried on one's person to assist in effecting whatever change is needed. There are many, many correspondence charts and books available to aid you in which crystals to use for which purpose; however, generally, color associations are useful—for example, green stones are great for prosperity and health.

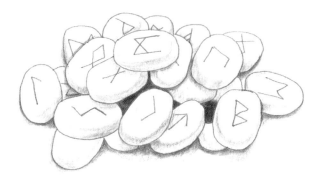

Candles

Candles are useful to every witch—from celebratory rituals to magical workings, candles are often involved in most aspects of what we do. White tapers and votives are good "go to" candles when you are not sure which color to use. Having a variety of colored candles on hand can also be useful—I will discuss the meanings of various colors in the chapter on spell workings.

A Bookshelf or Bookshelves

We Wiccans are a bookish lot—we love to read and study, and thankfully there are many publishers producing volumes that we love to read. Of course, you can read as much as you like, but also make sure you are actually DOING SOMETHING magickally. See below!

Deity Representations

These items are not absolutely necessary, but they are very nice to have if you happen to have deities with whom you specifically like to work with. There are many beautiful, affordable statues that have been created in recent years that it make it possible for Wiccans of any means to have nice representations of god and goddess on their altars. Again, I have included resources for where you can find these things in the index.

Yourself

I may have mentioned this already, but truly the most important magical tool you have is yourself and your brain! You can have all the beautiful, glittery implements in the world, but if you have no imagination and no spark of inspiration, none of them will work. A witch can create magic with nothing but his or her mind. Never forget that you are the one who puts everything into motion.

Mind Your Ps and Qs: Wiccan Etiquette

Circle Etiquette

If your mama raised you right, and you find some of this advice to be a bit repetitive of what you know to be correct, than please do not be offended. I am providing information here that may be useful, since being in Wiccan circles is not the same as attending parties, or possibly any other kind of event you may have been to. I hope that this will make some things clear and provide some guidance of what kinds of things to do and not do.

As I will be noting throughout this text, many traditions do things in different ways. If you attend an event at which a tradition that is different from yours is performing a ritual, it behooves you to be respectful of their choices. In other words, please do not attempt to correct them if they are assigning different elements to the quarters than you would choose—simply go with the flow. I promise you the ground will not open up and swallow you whole.

Once a circle has been cast in ritual, it is considered bad manners to come and go from the circle without knowing beforehand what that group's protocols are for such things. Some groups will not admit latecomers to circle at all, so in spite of what you might have heard about Pagan Standard Time, show up before the stated start time of any ritual. It is bad form to try to join a circle once it has begun. If this does happen to you, you may have to just wait to see if someone will "cut" you in.

What does "cutting in" entail? It is usually as simple as someone "cutting" a door in the circle energy, using an athame. They seal it up again once you are in the circle. The circle energy needs to remain intact—which is why having people just come and go as they please is considered bad form, and rude. If an emergency arises and you must leave the circle, once again, please find out who can cut you out of the circle. Most groups will have someone identified as the person to do this job before ritual.

Always move clockwise in the circle. Again, you will not be swallowed up whole by the ground if you move counterclockwise, but you will most likely bump into the other participants and, at the worst, annoy your hosts. There are occasions when it is appropriate to move counterclockwise, but do not do so unless instructed otherwise.

Another big issue is that of cell phones. I never would have thought I'd ever have to say this, but after several experiences taught me otherwise—do not bring your cell phone into circle and, for the love of the gods, PLEASE put it on silent if you must have it with you or if the ritual is occurring in the same room as your phone. There is nothing so distracting as hearing the phone ring in the middle of ritual. This is along the same line as please do not smoke while in ritual. This is another thing I never thought I would have to say; however, humans prove me wrong more often than not!

For the love of the gods, please do not touch things on an altar unless you are specifically invited to do so. Yes, it looks beautiful, and the high priestess probably took a lot of time creating it—tell her so, rather than putting your mitts on those sacred objects.

Festival and Conference Etiquette and Tips

There are many, many multiday pagan festivals and conferences across the United States and Europe, and I heartily encourage you to attend one (or more) if you have the opportunity. Festivals and conferences are a great way to get to know other pagans, hear your favorite writers speak, learn about other traditions, and pick up new skills. These events attract people from far and wide, and they usually have their guidelines in the guidebooks they publish for the event. Please be sure to read these, and also bear in mind a few of the following pointers in case they are not covered by the event itself.

Personal Space

Wiccans and pagans tend to be very friendly, loving people who want to hug everyone, new and old friends. Sometimes people forget that not everyone wants to be so readily embraced. Always ask before you go in for a hug, and do not hug someone who is not interested in a hug. Some people find a big hug from a stranger intimidating, or they come from a culture where there isn't a lot of public display of affection. In the worst-case scenario, the person is an abuse survivor who isn't ready to allow in new people. The reason doesn't really matter; please respect their wishes.

Sharing Sleeping Space

Some conferences take place in hotels, where everyone will have reserved their own rooms beforehand and will know who is staying where. In the case of festivals, people are usually sleeping in cabins, in which case they are most often sharing a cabin with people they may or may not know. In both of those cases, please be kind to your roommate(s) if you have them. Particularly in cabins, there are some people who don't seem to know how to respect personal space or personal belongings. This includes being neat, and not taking over the room with your stuff. I once shared a hotel room with someone I did not know who came from out of town, and I arrived at the conference a day later than she had. When I stepped into the hotel room for the first time, I was rather astonished to find she had taken over the entire room with all of her belongings, including the bed I was to sleep on. Fortunately, she was very nice and cheerfully removed her items from the space I was to use, but it helps if one doesn't have to have this conversation in the first place.

Eat, Sleep, Hydrate

This is not etiquette related so much as it is self-care related. At conferences and festivals, it is so exciting to meet new people interested in the same things as yourself, and to get so swept up in all the activities that you forget to look after yourself. There is definitely something known as "con drop" or "festival drop" that happens after you are home from one of these events and no longer in a 24/7 magickal environment. Eating, sleeping, and hydrating during the conference or festival helps keep that drop from being too harsh. It also will make you much more alert and able to absorb the new knowledge that you are taking in. Additionally, there is another phenomenon known as "con-crud," particularly at hotel events where people are in close quarters for a period of time. Stock up on your vitamins and elderberry syrup when you are at an event!

In Summation:

There are really so very many things you may want to have among your personal magickal stash that it would be impossible to list them all here. What I have listed here may give you a few ideas of the kinds of things you may want to start thinking about if you haven't already.

As for etiquette in getting out and working with your fellow witches and pagans, try to remember the golden rule, and the basic manners your mother taught you. Always be a good guest and a gracious host.

CHAPTER FIVE

THE WHEEL OF THE YEAR

he Wiccan Wheel of the Year is made up of eight holidays —two solstices, two equinoxes, and four "Cross Quarter" days, two of which are considered to be "High Holy Days." Each reflects the cycles of the seasons, the waxing and waning of light and dark in the earth, seen as a kind of balance, not as a polarized duality.

Because these eight holidays are based on the ancient European calendars, nearly all of them could be considered fertility rituals of a kind, since the ancients were very concerned with ensuring fertility and the continuance of the people. The timing of the rituals, as well, was dependent on geographical location—for example, winter occurs earlier in the British Isles than it does in our area. A number of the festivals also involve fire—nearly all Celtic celebrations involved fire of some sort.

Samhain

October 31, November 1. Halloween, Hallowmass, Hallow's Eve, All Soul's Day. Considered a High Holy Day

Samhain (pronounced "Sow-en") is considered the Celtic New Year's Eve, and it is also the third of three autumnal harvest festivals. At this time, all remaining crops and livestock must be harvested to be stored for the winter. This is a time of year when the veils are very thin, and it is easier for communication to

take place between this world and the Otherworld. Because of this, it is also a good time for divination. It is considered an in-between time, a moment that belongs to neither past nor present, to neither this or the Otherworld. Samhain is Gaelic for the month of November, and Samhuin is Scottish Gaelic for All Hallows, November 1.

The word "Samhain" means "summer's end" in Gaelic and marks what is sometimes also termed the "dark" half of the year, since the weather turns colder and preparations are made for the winter to come. The bones of the cattle that had been slaughtered would be cast upon the bonfires. Samhain was the time for slaughtering cattle to ensure there would be food during the colder months.

Because the veils between the worlds are thin during Samhain, it is a time when many Wiccans honor their ancestors and use this time to commune with them in ritual. There are many ways this can happen. Some have a "dumb supper" in which a plate and chair are left open for an ancestor, and no words are spoken during the meal. Others may try a more direct communication through a medium in ritual, or individually in meditation. It is a great time to build an ancestor's altar by allowing all coven members to bring photos and small items to ritual to create the altar together.

With the veils thin, Samhain is also a great time for divination. Since many neopagans celebrate Samhain as the new year, many people like to add some form of divination to their rituals, whether in the form of Tarot or rune readings, scrying, or pendulum work.

Yule

Winter Solstice, December 21

The Norse word *iul* means "wheel," which is central to the concept of this holiday. The Wheel of the Year turns again, and we find ourselves at the winter solstice. This concept also comes into play with one of the myths most associated with this holiday—the exchange of power at the solstices between the Oak King—the god of the waxing year, and the Holly King—the god of the waning year. In some stories, they battle one another at each solstice for the hand of the goddess, and the right to claim sovereignty over the year. The vanquished king goes back into the cosmos (perhaps back to the womb of the goddess, or to Caer Arianrhod) to await being called forth again at the next solstice.

The goddess is present at this time in her aspect of the Leprous White Lady—referring to how people who have survived leprosy appear to have very white skin. This refers to the way in which everything is stripped away in the winter—leaves from trees, the grass from the ground, and so on. The goddess is the queen of the cold darkness, yet she gives birth to the Child of Promise—the sun. He is the son/lover who will refertilize her and bring back the warmth and the light (these stories echo earlier myths of Isis and Osiris, of Ishtar and Tammuz).

Yule

The yule log represented the Sabbath fire being brought inside. A bonfire would take place at Yule, and one log would be preserved from the fire to be brought forth in the next year's bonfire—for the continuance of bringing back the warmth. Yule is also a time for letting go of grief and sorrow so that new things (such as the solstice sun) may come into our lives.

Traditions that prefer not to have battles in ritual have many other options. Those with a Hellenistic bent may mark this time with rituals centered on the seasonal Greek myth of Demeter and Persephone, in which Persephone enters the Underworld to be with her husband, Hades, for one-half of the year, while Demeter the Earth Goddess presides over the barrenness of the earth, waiting for her daughter to return. This can also be a time when the emphasis is placed on finding the solar fire within one's self and carrying that warmth within one's self for the colder part of the year.

Imbolg

Brighid/Oimelc/Candlemass, February 1, 2

From the Irish, we have the word *imbolg*, which means "in the belly." This is the perfect term to refer to this holiday, which is all about the growing things that can't yet be seen, growing deep in the Earth, in the belly of the goddess. Another term used for this holiday is the Irish *oimelc*, meaning ewe's milk, referring to the fact that soon the ewes will be giving birth to their lambs. For many living in the United States, February is often the harshest of the winter months, and this holiday serves to remind us that even in deepest, darkest winter, there is still the promise of life.

This holiday is also sometimes referred to as "Brighid" or "Bride's Day" in reference to the Celtic goddess whose feast this is. Brighid is a threefold goddess, and not in the way of maiden, mother, and crone, as is frequently held in pagan circles. Brighid is the threefold goddess of healing, poetry, and smithcraft, which can be interpreted as healing, inspiration, and the arts (as such, she is a favorite of mine). She is also associated with sacred wells and fires.

We know that Imbolg was important to the Irish because there are a number of megalithic and Neolithic sites where the light of the rising sun is aligned with tomb passages on Imbolg and Samhain. At the Loughcrew burial mounds and the Mound of the Hostages in Tara, Ireland, the rising Imbolg sun shines down a long shaft in the tomb and lights up the interior.

The holiday is a festival of the hearth and home, and a celebration of the lengthening days and the early signs of spring. Rituals often involve hearth fires, special foods, divination or simply watching for omens (whether performed in all seriousness or as children's games), a great deal of candles, and perhaps an outdoor bonfire if the weather permits.

Some people see the fierce goddess Cailleach—a one-eyed crone—as the dark counterpart to Brighid, and a goddess of the cold, dark winter. Brighid comes in at this time of year to remind us that although winter is not yet over, spring will be here soon.

Spring Equinox / ☉stara

Easter, Eastre, Oestre, March 21

With the spring equinox, the seeds that were beginning to germinate underground during Imbolg can now burst through the ground into full bud and bloom. The holiday of Easter gets its name from the Teutonic goddess of spring and the dawn, whose name is spelled Oestre or Eastre (the origin of the word "east" comes from various Germanic, Austro-Hungarian words for dawn that

share the root for the word "aurora," which means " to shine"). Modern pagans have generally accepted the spelling "Ostara," which honors this goddess as our word for the vernal equinox. The 1974 edition of *Webster's New World Dictionary* defines Easter thus: "orig., name of pagan vernal festival almost coincident in date with paschal festival of the church; Eastre, dawn goddess; 1. An annual Christian festival celebrating the resurrection of Jesus, held on the first Sunday after the date of the first full moon that occurs on or after March 21." The vernal equinox usually falls somewhere between March 19 and 22 (note that the dictionary mentions only March 21, as opposed to the date of the actual equinox), and depending on when the first full moon on or after the equinox occurs, Easter falls sometime between late March and mid-April. Because the equinox and Easter are so close, many Catholics and others who celebrate Easter often see this holiday (which observes Christ's resurrection from the dead after his death on Good Friday) as being synonymous with rebirth and rejuvenation: the symbolic resurrection of Christ is echoed in the awakening of the plant and animal life around us. But if we look more closely at some of these Easter customs, we will see that the origins are surprisingly, well, pagan! Eggs, bunnies, candy, Easter baskets, new clothes: all these "traditions" have their origin in practices that may have little or nothing to do with the Christian holiday. For example, the traditional coloring and giving of eggs at Easter has very pagan associations. Eggs are clearly one of the most potent symbols of fertility, and spring is the season when animals begin to mate and flowers and trees pollinate and reproduce. In England and northern Europe, eggs were often employed in folk magic when women wanted to be blessed with children.

The notion that one can balance an egg on end at the precise moment of the vernal equinox is actually an urban legend—it is possible to balance an egg on end anytime as long as you are careful. However, this urban legend reminds us of one of the other things this holiday is about—balance. The equinox denotes equal day and equal night. It is a good time to seek balance in one's life.

Once again, the myth of Demeter and Persephone may also come into play here, with Persephone's return to her mother, Demeter, bringing the joy of the flowers blossoming, leaves returning to trees, and the world turning green again after the cold, white winter. Some pagans also like to draw on the image of the egg as the symbol of new beginnings. In our modern times, the egg does not always have to represent physical fertility—it can represent abundance, prosperity, and, of course, starting anew.

Beltaine

May Day. May 1.

Beltaine (pronounced "Bell-tane") is at the opposite end of the wheel from Samhain—opposite ends of the Wheel of the Year: May 1 to November 1. There is an interesting celestial link to Beltaine, although it is a cross-quarter day, and not one of the solstices or equinoxes. At astrological Beltaine, the seven sisters of the Pleiades constellation rise just before sunrise. Samhain, on the other hand, sees the seven sisters rising just before sunset. If you are looking for the Pleiades in the night sky, they consist of a group of seven stars spaced closely together in the constellation of Taurus.

In ancient times, Beltaine and Samhain divided the year into the summer and the winter, respectively. Samhain and winter were considered to be the dark part of the year, and Beltaine and summer were considered to be the light part of the year. Since Samhain is about honoring our beloved dead, Beltaine, its counterpart, is about honoring life. Because it is a "between time"—marking the time between the waxing and the waning of the year—the veils between the worlds are at their thinnest at Beltaine and are thin again at Samhain, making Beltaine the second of our two high holidays.

There are many Celtic fire festivals, but Beltaine and Samhain are the most important. Essentially, Beltaine means "May Day" in Irish Gaelic, but it also refers to the god Bel, and the original meaning is Bel's fire. Bel is known by many variations of his name in ancient Gaelic, but today we'll be referring to him as the Roman Belenos.

Bel is known as "the Bright One," a solar god of light and fires. He is not strictly a solar god, since the Celts saw the sun as feminine. Belenos is similar to Cernunnos in that both are aspects of the Great Father who impregnates the Great Mother. Fertility and fire are two themes that dominate the Celtic holidays. There is also a corresponding goddess, Belisama, also a Roman-named Celtic deity. Her name literally means "Brightest One."

The ancient Celts celebrated Beltaine with the lighting of Bel fires on hilltops to celebrate the return of life and fertility. Cattle might be driven through the center of the fires for luck and to increase fertility. A few brave souls might try to leap over the fire for luck. Pregnant women might jump the fire to ensure a safe delivery; young people would jump it with the hopes of finding their future spouses.

The maypole is an important element to Beltaine festivities, since it is said to represent the ancient bile pole. The bile pole was a tree intended to honor the ancestors. Some people also liken the maypole and the bile pole to the World Tree. In some areas there are permanent maypoles, perhaps a recollection of the memory of ancient clan bile poles. In other areas, a new maypole is brought down on Beltaine Eve out from the wood. Even the classical wood can vary according to the area tradition is pulled from; most frequently it seems to be birch as "the wood," but others are mentioned in various historical documents.

The maypole also represents the fertility aspects of this holiday—the phallic pole is thrust into the fertile Mother Earth so that new life can come forth.

There are many stories of couplings taking place in the fields—helping to fertilize the new growth. I have heard it said that marriages took place traditionally in June because brides became pregnant at Beltaine.

If you yourself are not looking to become pregnant, Beltaine can instead be a time of metaphorical fertility—ask for blessings for new ventures, new projects, and your bank account.

Litha

Summer Solstice / Midsummer, June 21

The summer solstice is celebrated all over the world in many different forms and has been throughout history, going back to at least Neolithic times. The Celts, Norse, and Slavs believe that there are three nights in the year when the veils between this world and the Otherworld are at their thinnest: Samhain, Beltaine, and Litha, or midsummer. The summer solstice is the time when the faeries are the most active and the entrance to Otherworld is easiest found. The term "Litha" comes from the Saxons, who called the month of June *Aerra Litha*, meaning "before Litha." The term "Litha" itself is usually translated to mean either light or moon.

Litha is also the observance of the summer solstice—the longest day of the year—at the opposite of the winter solstice, the longest night of the year. The summer solstice marks the zenith of the sun and the longest hours of daylight. The word "solstice" comes from Latin and means "sun stand still." This refers to the sun appearing to rise and set in exactly the same place. The summer solstice appears in the constellation of Cancer the Crab. The sun seems to travel backward after this point in time every year—much in the way a crab appears to walk.

The Celts were so attached to the notions of the longest night and the longest day that they believed there were two suns—the sun of the waxing year and the sun of the waning year. This corresponds to Celtic stories of the Oak King and the Holly King battling for dominion at each solstice. The goddess remains constant at each solstice—it is the god who changes. Although the sun is at its height at this time, the year is now dwindling into winter, and it is the Holly King who holds sway. These polarities of light and dark, waxing and waning, are not polarities of good and evil, but rather polarities of balance—we cannot have one without the other.

Early humans tracked the phases of the moon and movement of the sun by making tallies on bones and sticks, and also marking the ground with pegs. During the megalithic and Neolithic periods, enormous stone circles were erected throughout northern Europe to mark the rising sun at the summer solstice. The Celts referred to these stone circles as "cromlechs"—Stonehenge is the most famous of all the cromlechs.

Gerald Gardner asserted that the solstices and equinoxes were the lesser holidays of the pagan Wheel of the Year, and that they were Middle Eastern imports. He believed that the holidays of Samhain, Imbolg, Beltaine, and Lughnasadh were of greater importance, and the solstices and equinoxes were later, less important additions to the wheel. Of course, this is shown not to be true, as evidenced by the proliferation of megalithic and Neolithic stone circles throughout the British Isles.

Litha is midsummer for the Celts, whose summer actually began on May 1, Beltaine. Celts, always fond of fire, made use of eight spoked fire wheels that they would light and roll down a hill. The midsummer fire itself was a major event. Each year, every village would have its own midsummer bonfire. The word "bonfire" may come from the term "boon fire"—basically a fire lit to ask the gods for the boon of a time of goodwill. The term might also come from the Norse word *baun*, meaning torch.

As the year was dwindling, the fire was used in rituals and spells for protection and prosperity. Rituals to ward off evil in all forms—whether human, spirit, or otherwise—would be conducted around the midsummer bonfire. The fire was also served as a ward against the more negative aspects of the approaching waning year: blight, hunger, death, and winter. Fire is the "little brother" of the sun—hence, the bonfires.

A midsummer fire had to follow certain standards. It had to be round and placed on a sacred spot near a holy well, a hilltop, or some other liminal site, such as a border or boundary. The boundary was entrance to and from the Otherworld.

As fire was important to midsummer, so was water. Wells and water figure prominently in a number of midsummer observances. For the Norse, it was the thunder god Thor, who brought the rains, which would help fertilize the land—much as the god fertilizes the goddess with his seed. Midsummer was a good time to make pilgrimages to holy wells in search of cures or to make offerings to the resident deity.

Because the veils are thin, midsummer is a wonderful time for magic. Healing, divination, and spells all can take on greater power at this time. Because of its relationship to fire, midsummer is an excellent time to create a wand. The midsummer sun imbues herbs with its healing and magickal properties.

Lughnasadh

Lughnasadh, Lammas, Loafmas August 1, Cross-Quarter Day

Lughnasadh means "commemoration of Lugh," who was the fire and light god of the Irish Tuatha de Danaan. He was a god of many skills, skilled at both arts and warfare. Lughnasadh falls opposite to Imbolg and is one of the four main fire festivals. The dates of these festivals may have varied slightly from year to year, since they were based on lunar, solar, and vegetative cycles. In Celtic mythology, the god Lugh created the holiday as a funerary feast and festival for his foster-mother Tailtiu. After clearing the fields of Ireland for planting, she died from exhaustion.

In English-speaking countries in the Northern Hemisphere, August 1 is Lammas Day (loaf-mass day), the festival of the first wheat harvest of the year. On this day it was customary to bring to church a loaf made from the new crop. In many parts of England, tenants were bound to present freshly harvested wheat to their landlords on or before the first day of August. In the Anglo-Saxon Chronicle, where it is referred to regularly, it is called "the feast of first fruits."

In keeping with the feast of the first fruits, many Wiccans and neopagans incorporate bread baking into their rituals. The kneading of bread is rhythmic, and chants can be sung while coveners work together to prepare the bread for cooking. The bread is put into the oven—like a sacrificial god—and when it comes out, the delicious warm bread can be shared and enjoyed.

In addition to bread, beer is also considered to be a product of the first-fruits harvest, and the traditional song "John Barleycorn" is often sung or played at Lammas/Lughnasadh rituals. John Barleycorn himself is also seen as a sac-

Lughnasadh

rificial god—transforming from wheat into ale. The beer also goes very well with the freshly baked bread coming out of the oven.

Mabon

Mabon is the name used by some Wiccans and other neopagans for one of the eight solar holidays or sabbats. It is celebrated on the autumnal equinox, which in the Northern Hemisphere occurs on September 23 (occasionally the 22nd, although many celebrate on the 21st) and in the Southern Hemisphere is around March 21. The name may derive from Mabon ap Modron, although the connection is unclear. Modron is the Welsh mother goddess, whose son, Mabon, was "stolen from between her and the wall when he was but three days old." A tale from the Mabinogian tells of an Arthurian quest in search of Mabon. Among the sabbats, it is the second of the three harvest festivals, preceded by Lammas and followed by Samhain.

Once again with the equinox, we come into the time of perfect balance. It is at this time the sun truly rises in the east and sets in the west, and the point at which we can observe the most rapid change in the sun's apparent motion. It is now that the nights dip into the "below freezing" temperatures, while the days can still be warm and delightful, and the trees increasingly change into their finest fall colors. It is as if at Mabon, the harvest erupts with overwhelming abundance, symbolized by the horn of plenty—the cornucopia brimming with bounty. The full moon closest to the equinox is known as the harvest moon, for the simple reason that the full moon enabled folks to work into the night, harvesting by its gentle light. If the full moon closest to the autumnal equinox is actually in November, then the September moon is typically named the corn moon.

Many Wiccans and neopagans think of Mabon as our Thanksgiving and have a feast at this time. It is not unusual for covens to have potlucks at this time in which everyone contributes to the meal, often with traditional foods such as meat pies, hams, roasts, potato cakes, cheeses made from spring's milk, custards, cakes, fresh fruit tarts and pies, corn bread, and cider. Typical fruits of this time are apples, cranberries (original name crane-berries—named for the cranes in the marshes where cranberries grow), fen-berry (the American cranberry's English cousin), grapes, hazelnuts, corn, squash, pears, and peaches.

It is a time of great joy and great sorrow; it is the time of great change. Mabon is as much about life as it is about death; it is the reminder that within life there is death, and within death there is life. It is about the dance that partners life with death.

Personal Work

Planning

A nice way of acknowledging and preparing for the coming year is to look up the astrological dates for each sabbat (they may be different from the calendar dates people celebrate most regularly) and add them to your planner. Take note of which sign the moon is in for each of those dates, and how that can affect the energies of that day.

A Meditation on the Wheel of the Year

Now that you have spent time reading about the Wheel of the Year, here is a meditation to further help your understandings of the year become clearer.

Take a few moments to ground and center yourself. Breathe in, breathe out, and as you exhale, let go of any tensions you may be holding in your body. With each outward breath, feel the troubles of the day leaving you. Feel yourself rooted to the Mother Earth . . . and turn inward. Turn to that place inside you where you connect with the Divine. Know that while you are within, there is nothing that can harm you.

You are standing on a wheel, a great wheel. Once again, you are on the Wheel of Time and Place. This great wheel corresponds to a great many things, but today you will be walking the Wheel of the Year. This great wheel has many concentric circles within it. As you stand where you are today, at the center, you can see the markings of the four elements, with Spirit in the center. The time comes to move outward to the part of the wheel that has eight markers going around it. They move up like doors spanning around the circle in eight different directions. You sense light beginning to stream out below one of the doors, and you head toward that door.

The door begins to open, and as it does, you can feel the heat of a large bonfire whush out toward you. You can feel the energy of the fire, and the many spirits who have gathered around it. The spirits dance around the fire, and some seem to look longingly toward the door, wishing to be reunited with their loved ones among the living. Perhaps your own ancestors are among these spirits. Stand silently for a moment, as inwardly as for one to come forward. When they do, greet them, thank them for coming, and ask them what they have to tell you about Samhain. When you have learned all that you can, the time comes to move on, and you go back through the door, onto the wheel, and move on to the next door . . .

The next door opens, and instead of heat, you feel the chill coming from a snow-filled field. Instead of the roar and energy of the fire, you hear only silence and feel the briskness of the cold air. The lonely cry of a raven hangs in the air. This place feels so cold, dark, and lonely. Soon, however, you see a light peaking out on the horizon. The sun is slowly coming up over a hill in the distance, and as it rises, it transforms and turns into a radiant child, who is now walking toward you. Here is the newly born Sun King. Greet him and thank him for coming. Ask him what he can tell you about Yule. . . . when you have learned all that you can, the time comes to move on, and you go back through the door, onto the wheel, and move on to the next door . . .

This door opens, and the chill of cold still hangs in the air. However, there is a bonfire blazing next to a well, and a woman . . . no, a goddess, really . . . stands next to the well. She beckons you to come forth. She is the goddess Brighid, appearing to you in one of her three forms—Goddess of Healing, Goddess of Inspiration, or Goddess of the Arts. Which one is she for you? Thank her for coming and ask her what message she has for you about Imbolg. . . . When you have learned all that you can, the time comes to move on, and you go back through the door, onto the wheel, and move on to the next door . . .

When this door opens, you finally feel a warm spring breeze brush past you as you walk through it into a beautiful, sunlit, colorful garden, full of beautiful blossoms and newly born animals playing. Another radiant goddess approaches you, her hair crowned with flowers. She is the Germanic goddess Eostre, and she welcomes you into the spring. Greet her and thank her for coming. Ask her what message she has for you about Ostara. . . . When you have learned all that you can, the time comes to move on, and you go back through the door, onto the wheel, and move on to the next door . . .

This door opens before you even reach it, and you hear laughter, music, and merriment through the opening. You walk through and find yourself in an open field, at the center of which is a large tree, crowned with a thistle and many ribbons, which are being spun around and woven by an odd number of dancers. One of them, upon seeing you entering the scene, says, "Please join us! We have room for one more!" You pick up the one remaining ribbon and begin the dance, which is joyful, and the music you hear is a tune that you love. You laugh as you hear the familiar melody and watch your feet below and the ribbons above as they weave a basket of color around the tree. In the center of the circle, as you and the dancers move closer and closer in the dance, suddenly Bel and Belisama appear, the brilliant countenances almost blinding with light. All dancing ceases while they greet all of you and thank you for coming. Listen now to the message they have to impart. . . . When you have learned all that you can, the time comes to move on, and you go back through the door, onto the wheel, and move on to the next door . . .

The next door turns into a boulder, one that allows you entry into a stone circle. Once again, you see the sun rising, and you see it perfectly framed between two of the stones as its light also beams down onto you. It is warm, and strangely silent after the noisy joy of Beltaine. The child who was the rising sun at Yule is now a much-older man, and he comes to you through the stones, to speak to you of the wisdom of Litha. Greet him and thank him for coming and allow him to tell you all that he can about this holiday. . . . When you have learned all that you can, the time comes to move on, and you go back through the door, onto the wheel, and move on to the next door . . .

Through this new door, you can smell the delicious scent of baking. You enter the door and find yourself in a labyrinth, constructed entirely of tall sheaves of wheat. You have nowhere to go but through this labyrinth, making your way through its twists and turns. At its center, there is a god lying on a stone table, as though he were dead. Standing at his head is a duplicate god—standing strong, tall, and alive and grasping a spear. He is the god, he of the Long Arm, he of the many talents. Greet him and thank him for coming, and ask him to tell you about the meaning of Lughnasadh. . . . When you have learned all that you can, the time comes to move on, and you go back through the door, onto the wheel, and move on to the next door . . .

You have come nearly full circle, but there is still one more door to enter. A tall woman opens the door and bids you enter. She tells you she is the Corn Mother, and you have arrived in time for her great feast. She leads you to a great table, laden with many foods of all kinds, all the things that have been harvested since Lughnasadh. She welcomes you in and bids to you partake of the feast. She tells you all about the autumnal equinox, equal day and equal night, and of the blessings that come with this day. . . . When you have learned all that you can, the time comes to move on, and you go back through the door, onto the wheel . . .

Look out now at all of the places where there were doors on the wheel, and you can now see faint scenes of each holiday unfolding in each of those spots. Remember all that you have seen, and come back now, into your own body, and back into the present moment. Write down any new insights into your journal.

CHAPTER SIX

ESBATS AND THE MOON

he moon has long held a fascination for all kinds of people from ancient times. Lunar energy is said to be more feminine and aligned with goddess energy, although honestly, on occasion, one finds the moon to be masculine in a few pantheons. Science has documented the many ways in which the moon influences the Earth, from ocean tides to human moods and women's menstrual cycles. Taking note of the cycles of the moon is very useful in magic, and each phase of the moon has qualities that work well for different magical purposes.

The Esbats

Esbats are rituals that occur on the full moon. Not all witches celebrate the full moon each time it occurs; some witches prefer to hold new-moon rituals, and some like to work with both at different times, depending on their needs. (The idea of holding ritual at the full moon is found in the Charge of the Goddess: "Whenever you have need of anything, once a month, and better it be when the moon is full, you shall assemble in some secret place and adore the spirit of Me Who is Queen of all the Wise.") The phases of the moon correspond to the faces of the goddess—maiden, mother, and crone. Some witches like to celebrate the moons according to their Celtic names, while some like to use other names, corresponding to animal totems or some other traditional name.

Each month finds the moon occurring in a different sign, and it is helpful if you are going to be working with lunar energies to know the effect the moon has when it is in different signs. It is easy enough to find an online ephemeris to tell you not only which phase the moon is in, but also which sign it is occupying at the time. This can have an effect on the kind of magic you may wish to do during an esbat.

An important thing to know in any month is when the moon is considered to be "void of course." The moon goes void of course every two days; when it has made its last major aspect to a sign, the moon is then not in any sign for a period of time. This period of time may be for several minutes or within several hours. Avoid doing any magic when the moon is void of course. Thankfully, this rather difficult time is short, because it is a bad time to try to focus and make decisions, since they may prove unfruitful. Again, you can find out when the moon will be void of course each month by consulting an ephemeris online.

Phases of the Moon

The New Moon

New-moon energies are best for workings in which you are trying to begin something new or attract new energies to yourself. In this phase, the moon is the maiden aspect of the goddess. After the moon moves into a new phase, it begins to wax, or appear to grow bigger in the sky. During the waxing moon is the best time to do magical work when you want to attract or increase something, such as looking for a job or a partner, or trying to increase your income.

The full moon corresponds to the mother aspect of the goddess. You will want to check an astrological calendar or an online moon tool to determine when the moon will be the most full. To take full advantage of the full moon, be sure to begin your working an hour or two prior to the moon being "officially" full—once the moon becomes full, it begins to wane once again.

There is much discussion in some of the more traditional literature about witches going to meetings at the full moon in black capes and meeting secretly—which certainly corresponds to Doreen Valiente's Charge of the Goddess. However, the full moon can be what you need it to be. It is always best if a ritual can be held outdoors so that all may admire the beauty of the full moon, but weather and privacy do not always allow for this. One should at least make an effort to try to look at the full moon in all of her beauty for at least a few minutes, even if ritual must be held inside.

In the tradition I was trained in, important initiations took place on the full moon, at an auspiciously astrological time when the transits were favorable to whatever effect we wanted the ritual to have on the initiate. In yet other traditions, there is a magical rite known as "Drawing Down the Moon," in which the energy of the lunar goddess is drawn down into a priestess, who embodies the goddess for a time.

A practice that some witches like is the creation of "moon water." When the moon is about to be full—and you will want to check an ephemeris or online source for the exact time—set out a bowl of water to catch the reflection of the full moon and catch its energies. You can use this water for purification, blessing, etc.

The Dark Moon

Some people view the new moon and the dark moon synonymously, but there is a difference between the waxing and waning moon. When the moon is moving toward being full, it is waxing; when it has completed the full part of the cycle, it is waning. Check an almanac or online tool to be certain of which is which. The dark moon corresponds to the crone aspect of the goddess and is a good time for ridding yourself of things—banishing depression, or for dealing with endings of all kinds. There are some who associate the dark moon with "sinister" magic, with curses and the like, but that is not the only thing shadow is for. We need both dark and light, and when we understand the dark, we can better appreciate the light, and as witches, it helps to understand both. The key is to know what is ethical and unethical, and to use one's discernment and judgment when choosing the kind of magic to work.

Lunar Eclipses

A lunar eclipse can occur only when the moon is full. You do not have to be able to see the moon to work with full-moon energy, so you can still do magical workings. I have read some articles online stating that doing magick during an eclipse is dangerous; however, I have never found that to be the case. What I have found is that the energy is magnified by the eclipse, and whatever you do gets a bit of a boost.

Drawing Down the Moon

In the Gardnerian tradition, this ritual is performed when a priest draws down the power of the moon into the high priestess through the recitation of a poem. The high priestess enters into a trance, and the energies of the moon enter her body. Once the ritual is performed, any words or actions taken by the high priestess are considered to be those of the goddess herself. The nature of this

experience is not unlike spirit or trance possession or even mediumship. The person who acts as goddess will not retain any memory of words spoken or action taken. In the tradition I was trained in, we did not perform this exact ritual; however, we had another method for enacting divine embodiment through a process called aspecting.

Other groups have used aspecting as a term for a similar process—in some cases, the individual may or may not recall what took place during their divine embodiment; however, in my former tradition the process was designed so that the human performing the process would not lose consciousness or complete control. Even with this process, there were times when it was difficult for people to always remember precisely what may have been said while in aspect, perhaps for the reason that it is difficult for humans to retain this kind of energy for long periods of time.

I personally do not believe that it is always necessary for one individual to call forth deity to embody another person, although it can be helpful at times when the person in question is not very experienced in these kinds of techniques. Going into trance can be achieved through a number of means—through listening to a repetitive drumbeat, listening to music, chanting, or dance. There are also differing levels of trance, from a light trance to a very deep state of trance.

Why does one need to be in a state of trance in order to perform this activity? It is because our ego, our everyday consciousness, needs to be moved aside so that you can be open to receive messages. Ideally, you will have already established a daily meditation practice so that you are already somewhat familiar with methods for achieving different states of consciousness. If not, it is never too late to begin meditating, and if you think can't meditate, please move ahead to chapter 9 and read all about it before attempting to draw down.

When doing this for the first time, although I have said it is not necessary to have another individual draw the moon down into you, you may wish to have a friend present to aid you in grounding and centering before and after the rite, and also to help record your experience of the event. You may also want to have your journal on hand, and maybe some tea and cookies to aid in grounding afterward.

Check an ephemeris or other astrological aid to find when the moon is full. The moon is technically considered for a particular period. For your purposes here, the best time to choose is shortly before the moon is completely full, with enough time to complete the rite before it is actually full. Once the moon becomes officially full, it begins to wane.

To begin, get yourself relaxed and calm. Call upon your guides and spirits to assist you in this work, and then get yourself into a meditative state in the fashion you like best. Invoke the goddess and ask her to be present. There have been many who have written invocations for this purpose, and you can certainly find and use one that you like. I will say, however, that words that come from your own heart will carry the most weight—it is emotion that makes the best magic. Whether you are inside or outside, it is most helpful if you are somewhere that you can see the moon. Raise your arms upward as if to embrace the moon into yourself. Speak again—words that come from your heart—and ask the moon to be present within you.

What happens next is different from person to person. You may feel a tingling in your head, or in your heart. You may feel your hands tingling. You may feel an actual presence, a sense that there is someone else looking out through your eyes. Some people remember their experiences, but most often they do not. This is why it is helpful to have a friend working with you. Pay attention to how it feels in your body, mind, and heart; there is a very distinct difference in drawing down from meditation.

While the goddess is embodied within you, you may receive messages that may come into your head, or that you will want to speak aloud. Your friend can jot down these things for you, or you can share and jot them down afterward. There is a definite energy surge that you can feel while the goddess is within you, and you will feel that subside after a little while. This is also where it is good to have a friend nearby the first time you attempt this. If you are "in" a little too long, your friend can help draw you back. Remember to ground thoroughly when you are finished. Feel yourself in your own body, your own skin. Touching the ground can help, as well as the Tree Meditation in chapter 9 for grounding and centering.

Moon Correspondences

The moon in the signs—what kind of workings to do!

MOON IN ARIES
When the moon is in Aries, the focus tends to be on one's self and one's goals. You may find that you and the people around you are impulsive and quick acting. Channel this energy into something of a creative project. It is also a time when you may want to be more active—perhaps doing a ritual involving movement of some kind.

MOON IN TAURUS

A Taurus moon tends to calm moods and has a stabilizing energy. It is a good time to be with the people you love. Taurus itself is ruled by Venus, the planet of beauty, so you may want to make any rituals you do extra beautiful—decorate your altars and home to please the eye.

MOON IN GEMINI

Talkative, brainy Gemini loves communication and new ideas. Moods tend to come and go quickly and may need some exploration and talking out. This is a good time for looking at what needs to be done and setting it into motion.

MOON IN CANCER

The moon actually rules Cancer and is very comfortable in this sign. People's emotions tend to take center focus and may require nurturing. This is a good time to see who or what needs a little extra love, even yourself. It is a good time to do rituals focused on the home.

MOON IN LEO

Fiery Leo loves attention and is very generous. It is a good time to work with others in ways that bring enjoyment. Creativity is also at an increase, so doing a creative project with other people will be productive and fun.

MOON IN VIRGO

Those with their sun sign in Virgo are said to be practical, neat, and exacting. When the moon is in this sign, it is a good time for practical work and paying attention to details. It is a good time to do more ceremonially oriented ritual.

MOON IN LIBRA

Libra loves harmony, balance, and beauty. Rituals involving finding the balance, attuning one's chakras, and somehow involving beauty will be more effective during this time. Libra wants everyone to get along, so doing group ritual with others of a like mind will go very well.

MOON IN SCORPIO

The moon in Scorpio can help bring out everyone's psychic sides. The mind is sharper and people are more attentive. Full-moon energies will intensify the moon in this sign, so this moon is a good time to do astral and psychic work.

MOON IN SAGITTARIUS

Sagittarius is a fire sign, which brings warmth and optimism to any working you may do. Because of its fiery and mutable nature, Sagittarius likes to move around a lot, so this is a good time for ritual involving dance. Additionally, Sagittarius's symbol is the centaur—a classical teacher; this is a good time for workshops and teaching others.

MOON IN CAPRICORN

Conservative, cautious Capricorn likes planning and strategy. This can be a good time to finish up projects that have already been started, and thinking about the future.

MOON IN AQUARIUS

The moon in Aquarius is long on ideas and intellect, but short on emotion. Working on something new and unusual is good at this time. Aquarius likes the unconventional.

MOON IN PISCES

Mutable water sign Pisces is emotional and unpredictable and enjoys flights of fantasy. It may actually be difficult to concentrate, so focus on things that are calming and active at the same time, such as art projects and making music.

CHAPTER SEVEN

YOUR RELATIONSHIP WITH THE GODS

Introduction

ne of the beautiful things about being Wiccan is also being a polytheist, or a pantheist. A polytheist believes in more than one deity, whereas a pantheist believes that there is divinity throughout the entire universe. As you become more familiar with Wicca and Wiccans, you will no doubt hear many personal stories from Wiccans about the gods and goddesses with whom they work.

Some Questions That May Arise for You

What are patrons? Must I choose my own patrons? Or will they somehow choose me? How will I know if I am chosen? What do I do if I hear the "call" of a particular god or goddess? Must I answer that call? What happens if I don't? May I choose a god or goddess from a pantheon from other than my own ancestral background? (for example, you are a nice Irish girl, but Elegba is calling you). What is respectful and what is cultural appropriation? Can't I just worship the god and goddess generically? Aren't all the gods one god?

Patron(s) is a term used by many neopagans and Wiccans to refer to the main deities with whom they work. Some people prefer to work only with their patrons, and some work with a variety of deities and pantheons. Some people have very close and devoted relationships with their patrons, which only they can describe. Fortunately, a number of people now blog regularly about their relationships with deity, and you can read/hear in their own words what those relationships are like.

There are those who will tell you that you may work only with deities from pantheons whose cultures reflect your own ancestral heritage. Some will say that if you are a woman, you must choose a male patron, and if you are a man, you must choose a female patron. Some will tell you that you must have both a male and a female. Some people work with a variety of different gods throughout their lives with no ill effect at all, and others insist that they can work with only one or two gods, or only with a specific pantheon. Every individual is different, every relationship will be different, and that also applies to our relationships with the gods.

What Is Deity?

Let's first take a look at what deity means. In the tradition I was trained in, we view deity from several different angles. At the broadest, most-open, and universal level, there is a universal energy that pulsates through everything that one might call God. However, this energy is so vast and so unindividualized that trying to send prayers its way is difficult at best—it tends to go off into the universe, only to not be answered.

At the next level, there are god/goddess types—archetypes, if you will. These are "big" energies, but with a bit more focus than praying to the all-encompassing universal life energy. These energies include father, mother, moon, sun, earth, and other natural forces. I was taught that there are nonhuman entities of this type that are interested in human development, who do wish to help us. A few examples will follow.

A moon goddess who may wish to be of assistance to humans may look down upon Earth and find she happens to like the image of the Greek Selene—a moon goddess. This energy finds this particular image suits her, so she will work with it and adopt that image. The same could be said for someone searching for a word with a sea deity—Manannan Mac Lir might come forward in that case. If someone prefers a sea deity with a feminine aspect, perhaps it would be Yemoja. In other words, deity finds its way to us through the "clothing" we humans provide for it. Having said that, there are many other variables such as culture, and the times in which one lives, and times in which the deity may have been recognized.

A god or goddess who has existed for a number of centuries and been worshiped in many cultures will have larger energies than one who was worshiped only in one place and one time period. For example, a goddess such as Isis was worshiped for thousands of years in ancient Egypt. The Romans eventually conquered Egypt, and they adopted many Egyptian practices, such as Isis worship, which they took with them into other parts of Europe, which is why one can find temples to Isis in Great Britain. Another example would be the Celtic Danu, whose worship was spread throughout Europe, and who has many places named after her; for example, the Danube River.

Whom to Choose? And How?

Some of us are fortunate and will have a strong pull toward a particular pantheon. Many Wiccans are drawn to the Celtic pantheon, which is wonderful since there is a lot of information available on the Celts. The Asatru have a very strong connection with their gods and are very thorough in their research of the existing literature. A thorough knowledge of the myths of a particular pantheon is crucial. Some pantheons are fairly peaceful and have good relationships with one another. Other pantheons have gods and goddesses who are at odds with one another, and you want to know this so that you do not invoke deities who don't like each other into the same circle.

A friend once told me I should invoke Lakshmi, for creativity. I learned a few minutes later that I should NOT invoke Shakti at the same time (she is inspiration) because if I invoke one, the other won't show up. Lakshmi and Shakti are part of the Vedic (Indian) pantheon. I decided I liked less complicated deities. Having said that, I might want to read a little bit more about those two and their interactions. In some Santeria traditions, the ocean goddess Yemoja and the river goddess Oshun do not like one another. However, in their native Yoruban African setting, Yemoja and Oshun are just fine together.

Another issue that often arises is that of cultural heritage. There are those who believe that you may not choose a pantheon from whose heritage you can not claim ancestry. I wonder if anyone explained this to several African Americans I know who are very devoted Asatruars? My personal belief is that the gods will call whom they will, and that we are all truly related. Yoruba priestess Luisah Teish once told me that she felt our ancestors are angry with us for not getting along and are sending us to places we might not otherwise explore. Having said that, I do believe it is important to acknowledge the possibility of cultural appropriation.

To quote Bruce Ziff from the book *Borrowed Power: Essays on Cultural Appropriation*, "The term cultural appropriation has been defined as the taking—from a culture that is not one's own—of intellectual property, cultural expressions, or artifacts, history and ways of knowledge" (Ziff 1997, p. 1). This is a very broad definition—we as Americans would be guilty of cultural appropriation on many levels if we applied this definition to ourselves. In recent times, however, the issue of cultural appropriation has emerged at all levels of American culture—from the use of Indian names for athletic teams to the names of African tribes for cars. As such, it is a very touchy issue, and one that must be approached with caution. In 1994, members of the Lakota tribe actually declared war on New Age spirituality groups for behaving as "wannabes." For peoples who are often oppressed by the dominant culture, seeing members of that culture appropriate their spiritual traditions as their own can be painful and horrifying at worst. Things become more confusing when we learn of Native American elders who are passing their knowledge along to Caucasians for the sake of allowing their spirituality to continue, by whoever wishes to practice it. I am also reminded of the Chinese invasion of Tibet—if the Chinese had not invaded Tibet, the Tibetan Buddhist monks might not have ever left their monasteries to share knowledge of their religion with the world.

How then may we, as responsible and caring people, approach this issue, particularly when we feel a call from a pantheon that does not echo our own ancestral heritage? First, there must be an acknowledgment that at some level, there will most likely always be those who will object. Second, it must be remembered that we must be responsible and respectful. It goes back again to the question of fully researching whichever culture a particular deity comes from, and being respectful to that culture. We must not seek to romanticize whatever culture we are researching with the notion that its ideals and aims are somehow purer and nobler than our own. We must realize that all paths are sacred and that humans created all paths, and that humans are flawed.

I found a wonderful quote on the Breathless Noon website:

The majority of spiritual seekers in North America are white, heterosexual, middle-class individuals, and as such, most have no real understanding of what it means to be a minority, to be in danger of losing one's culture and/ or community. It is difficult for many of us to understand that no one is entitled to the practices and ceremonies of other peoples. No one is entitled to free access to the inner workings of any religious and/or cultural society. (http://www.breathlessnoon.com/index.php)

I believe we must always remember to acknowledge where we found something, and to pay it homage. I believe that we can take inspiration from other cultures, but we must acknowledge that and pursue our beliefs in ways that do not damage or threaten existing cultures who may carry these same beliefs. I do believe this is possible—but it is essential to respect wherever you got whatever it is you have found, and to acknowledge it and acknowledge that you yourself are not a part of that culture.

Research, Research, Research!

If you feel drawn to a particular pantheon, be sure to research it as thoroughly as possible—spend time reading whatever literature is available; in particular, literature known as "first sources," if it is available. This means finding literature that was either written by the ancient worshipers themselves, if they were literate, or finding the best translations available. A Greek scholar once explained to me that the difference between a good translation and a bad translation can be "the rosy-tipped fingers of dawn" versus "the sun came up."

The best research is done at your library or bookstore. Don't rely on the internet for accurate information. There are some websites that may be trusted; however, since the internet is not refereed, we simply cannot rely on it for good information. You also want to be choosy about the books you read. As I mentioned earlier, try to seek out "first sources." If you are not sure what these are, talk with a more experienced friend or read the bibliographies of books you find in the library. Often one good source will turn up another. You can use the annotated bibliography at the end of this book as a tool in your research.

Some cultures did not have the benefit of a written language. The Celts, although highly intelligent, with their brehon system of law, did not have a written language. Instead, bards were trained in memorization and told stories that were passed down generation to generation, town to town. This is very common throughout Africa as well. What these cultures lack in what we Westerners think of as literacy, they more than make up for in skills involving memory and storytelling.

In cases like these, what unfortunately happened is that the stories were eventually written down . . . by someone else. In the cases both of the Celts and the Norse, the old sagas and tales were written down by Irish monks sometime around the seventh through tenth centuries. Much of what we know about Celtic and Norse culture before that time was written down by the Romans—who were trying to conquer these people and may not have always recorded them in the most flattering light. In the case of the Norse sagas and Celtic tales, some elements of the old stories have been lost or told in a light that is far more Christian. In cases like these, we must do our best to separate the wheat from the chaff.

There is something else the Romans did that has forever affected the way we look at mythology in the West. The Romans really liked everything—whether an aqueduct, the Roman Senate, or their mythology—to be very neat and orderly, and for like things to correspond to like things in a logical way. The Romans applied this to their myth structure, starting with when they appropriated Greek gods and goddesses and gave them Roman names. As the Romans conquered their way across Europe, they did their best to assimilate the local deities with their own, which is how we have compound deities such as Minerva Sulis (a combo Roman/Celtic goddess) and gods such as Cernunnos—a compound of all Celtic horned deities neatly tied up into one horned god. Sadly, this approach has tumbled over into the way we approach pantheons in modern times.

Many magical books will have lovely correspondence tables in which there will be a list of moon goddesses, a list of sun gods, and so forth. Not all pantheons are so neatly ordered. Many pantheons have gods and goddesses who have numerous attributes and do not fit neatly at all into the generic "god of love" or "god of war" category. Most pantheons have more-subtle and more-complex relationships within their gods and goddesses. The more reading and research you do, the better these relationships and subtleties will come through for you.

The Dreaded Unsubstantiated Personal Gnosis!

What do you do if you come across a god or goddess that you feel a connection to, and about whom there is very little written information? This is an excellent question, and also one that has caused some controversy in the form of something known as the UPG—the unsubstantiated personal gnosis. Let's say one day you've discovered you have a connection with a little-known goddess from

a little-known culture, and you sit down one day to meditate upon her. You have the most wonderful meditation, one in which the goddess not only reveals herself to you but also reveals information about herself that has not been recorded anywhere, and there is nothing written anywhere to back up what you have experienced.

There are those who look very unkindly on the UPG and would not accept anything that came from a UPG under any circumstances. Wicca does tend to be more forgiving; however, you should always proceed carefully. If possible, try to find out what you can about that particular deity from what is written, and use your UPG to supplement that information. You may wish to limit who you share this information with—as I've mentioned, there are those who look very unfavorably upon the UPG. Having said that, however—it is YOUR relationship with the deity in question, and your personal experience—it is up to you to interpret it and do what you will with it. Do not try to put forth this information as something that is written in stone: UPGs are just that—PERSONAL. Someone else may have an entirely different experience with the same deity. However, if you like fighting with strangers on the internet, UPG seems to be a great topic for stirring things up!

As a Wiccan, you will most likely find yourself working with different deities toward different purposes, whether those purposes are magickal or celebratory. If you are working with a coven, the deities invoked at each ritual may vary, especially if that group is eclectic, as many modern pagans are. How, then, to choose deity for ritual?

In my experience, it has always made the most sense to try to be consistent with pantheons within a particular ritual. In other words, don't mix and match from vastly different traditions. If you choose a Welsh god, choose a Welsh goddess. This also brings us back to compatibility—do research to ensure that the deities you are invoking actually like one another. Wicca does tend to be more forgiving than other paths, and the sky won't cave in if you make a mistake, but your rituals and magick are more likely to function well if you work with deities who are compatible.

If you are doing celebratory rituals for specific sabbats, it helps to call upon gods and goddesses who have specific connections to those holidays. Once again, research is your friend here. There seems to be no end to online lists of gods and goddesses for this or that purpose, so dig a bit more deeply and see what really works for you. If you are doing specific magick toward a specific end (for example, finding a job), you may wish to call upon a god or goddess from your chosen pantheon who would be effective in helping you with that task.

Patrons/Patronesses

Is it necessary for you to have your own personal patrons with whom you have a relationship? Once again, different people will answer this differently, but I personally find having a relationship with a particular deity very satisfying and helpful. I have considered Isis a personal patron for years, and she certainly has been steadfast for me. I can't say for sure if she chose me or if I chose her. I do remember being enthralled and in love with photographs of Isis statues in my father's copy of the 1962 Tutankhamen exhibition catalog, which is where I first encountered her.

Having a relationship with a deity makes it easier when you need to call upon someone for assistance. There may be times when other patrons will appear in your life, for different reasons. When I first became pagan, my focus was almost exclusively Celtic. Isis has always somehow factored into my life, but I wasn't especially aware of her at that time. As I became more educated in Wicca and magick, she began to emerge more strongly for me as a patron. Sometimes, a patron will appear who may be in your life for a short period of time, for a specific reason. I have been working with Freya off and on; I went through years of relationship woes—something she understands—and am appreciative of her help.

Can You Have Patrons from More Than One Pantheon?

Confusingly, yes, you can! It happens! For a time, the Native American Kokopelli was one of my patrons. Right along with Egyptian Isis and Yoruban Yemaya. Sometimes, your patrons will appear out of what your needs are, and this doesn't always have much to do with a particular culture so much as what you are needing in your life.

At this point in your search, you may not have any idea who your patron/patrons is/are. That is perfectly fine. My advice is to do lots of reading and research until you find the patrons with whom you feel comfortable. Fear not the UPG and meditate on the god/goddesses you are interested in; see whom you feel comfortable with. Do beware cultural appropriation but do not fear exploration—remember the three Rs: research, respect, responsibility!

CHAPTER EIGHT

WITCHES AND ETHICS

itchcraft is both a science and an art, although many in the medical profession would disagree with me. I personally believe that a lot of things we currently think of as magick may eventually be things that are proven in science. We have seen this with chaos theory, and quantum physics is a field that always seems to be revealing theories that verge on the mystical. Witches are benders and shapers of energy; we are ofttimes working to change reality. Scientists and doctors have a set of ethics they must follow as they work on vulnerable human beings, animals, and the world around us. So must we.

For the longest time, the only guideline for ethics in Wicca seemed to be the Rule of Three, as well as "An it harm none, do as ye will." Both of these statements are somewhat vague. Will our actions truly be visited upon us three-fold? Why just threefold? What exactly does it mean to have something come back to us? Does it come back immediately? In another life? Do Wiccans view karma as other religions do? What exactly is harm? How can we know whether our actions have harmed another?

Another term that often comes up in discussions of ethics is "Perfect Love and Perfect Trust." Wouldn't it be wonderful if we lived in a world where we could always experience perfect love and perfect trust? This phrase is often uttered when we are asked by a priest or priestess, "How do you enter this circle?" When we reply, "In perfect love and perfect trust," we are promising to conduct ourselves with both perfect love and perfect trust. Many people have interpreted the phrase to imply that everyone in the circle has agreed to conduct themselves thus, and I would argue that is how it is supposed to be. However, the only people whose minds and intents we can truly know are our own, and

so we promise that we as individuals come to the circle in perfect love and perfect trust.

Most Wiccan traditions have taken those aforementioned statements to mean that one should NEVER curse or practice what is known as baneful magick. The definition of baneful magick is essentially magick of any kind that interferes with the will of another. You have probably heard the terms "white witch" and "black magick." Both of these are rather polarizing for several reasons, especially in the racially charged climate of the US. Most people these days avoid terms like that; however, they have been used as a way of differentiating witches from Satanists, or people whose practices included cursing and baneful magick. Even nowadays, many Satanists also have their own set of ethics and guidelines.

The kinds of magic that could harm others include the obvious, such as curses, spells meant to break up relationships, and spells meant to make others lose their jobs, but if we include the notion of interfering with the will of another, then it becomes more subtle and more complex. For example, love spells that are directed at a specific individual are not respecting that individual's personal will. It is acceptable to do a spell to bring more love into your life, or even to attract a particular KIND of individual. Additionally, in many traditions a simple binding (a spell that prevents someone from doing something) is considered to be baneful; however, if a binding is being done to protect one person from another who intends to do them harm, then it can be acceptable.

I must ask the reader to realize that I am speaking of my own opinions about these differences and subtleties. There are traditions that prohibit binding under any kind of circumstance. I tend to be of the opinion that if we are witches and we cannot do magic to defend ourselves and our loved ones, then what are we here for? However, others may not agree, so if you decide to join a group, do be sure of where they stand on ethics and certain kinds of activities.

The nuances and subtleties of differing beliefs also comes into play where healing is involved. I tend to agree with many of my colleagues on this one—if someone has not specifically asked you to perform a healing spell or to do healing for them, then please do not do it. There are a variety of reasons why this is so, and also why someone may not want lots of well-intended people shooting well-meaning energy at them all at once. Always ask people if they wish to receive healing. If you are in a position where the individual in need of healing is not Wiccan or pagan and would in fact be mortified if you asked if you could do a healing for them, then please honor their beliefs and leave them alone.

Having said all this, do I really think the gods would punish us for our good intentions? No, I do not—however, always try to make the best-informed decision possible given the circumstances. For example, sometimes healing is not possible. Really, it isn't—we live in a natural world where all things die, and sometimes a person simply comes to the end of their life through old age or through a terminal illness. If you find that you are really in a fix and are unsure of what to do, then I recommend praying for the very highest good as the outcome.

A takeaway that one may have from all of this is that consent is very important to Wiccans. This applies to healing, spell-crafting, and all areas of life. Our ethics are about how we treat ourselves, our world, and one another rather than hard-and-fast rules and "thou shalt nots." Many Wiccans and pagans are polyamorous—that is, we believe that it is perfectly ethical to have more than one person as our life partner, as long as everyone involved knows about it and consents to the relationship. Additionally, we do not give side eye or cast shade on those who may enjoy a great deal of sexual pleasure—once again, as long as everyone involved knows exactly what is happening and is consenting.

As has been noted elsewhere in this text, Wicca is a path of personal responsibility, and we realize that in the end, we answer to ourselves and to our gods. There is no belief in a personification of evil that leads the unwary astray, and we firmly believe that if we behave badly, we will experience a direct cause and effect from that behavior. We must always come from a place of asking what the final intended outcome will be, as well as what an unintended outcome could be.

CHAPTER NINE

PSYCHIC DEVELOPMENT AND DIVINATION

Note: I am deeply indebted to my friend Fred DiCostanzo for his assistance in discussing psychic development with me, with my students, and for this book.

here are a lot of books available today on divination—usually on specific forms of divination. Finding a general book is difficult, and finding the means you most like to use for divination can be difficult if you are not familiar with the practice.

According to the *American Heritage Dictionary*, divination is

The art or act of foretelling future events or revealing occult knowledge by means of augury or an alleged supernatural agency.

An inspired guess or presentiment.

Something that has been divined.

For Wiccans, divination is all of those things, but perhaps a bit more. Wicca is a religion, which is a loaded proposition for many people. Religion is perceived as a means of oppressing people (Marx said, "Religion is the opiate of the masses"), as a way for weak people to badger the Divine into giving them what they want, and all the other negative connotations that go along with that word. If we think of the less charged version of the word, religion is about a particular path one follows in accordance with one's spiritual beliefs. Where does divination fit within Wicca?

One of the ways in which people have traditionally communicated with the Divine is through divination. The term has come to also mean seeking knowledge of the future, sometimes through the Divine and sometimes through the spirit world. Most people use tools to assist them with divination, whether those tools are runes, Tarot cards, tea leaves, astrology, or cowry shells. These tools offer up symbol systems that allow for interpretation. There are also seers who are gifted enough to receive information without the means of these kinds of tools. We will explore both kinds of divination.

Whatever one's spiritual practice, it is crucial to have some kind of daily meditative practice. Meditation is truly the key to being able to achieve anything magickally, and it assists greatly with divination. Being able to clear the mind allows the practitioner to open channels that allow for communication. The other key is practice. The more you work with and develop your abilities, the more they will grow. If you choose to work with tools such as the Tarot and the runes, offer to do readings for your friends. I am sure they will gladly act as guinea pigs!

Divination is not about being able to "see the future"; it is more about gaining insights and tools into dealing with one's life. What is seen in a reading is not written in stone, for a variety of reasons. One of these reasons is free will. I might predict that John Smith will be offered a particular job, but John Smith might decide he doesn't want that job. There are all kinds of choices people make on a daily basis that open up what I call "windows of opportunity." Diviners do their best to see what these opportunities are, but due to choices made by the querent, and the people around him or her, those opportunities may change or even disappear altogether.

There are definitely ethical issues to consider in divination. Among them, do not do a divination on an individual unless they have asked. Just as you (one hopes) would not go rummaging through someone's underwear drawer, you should not be doing readings on someone who has no idea you are doing it. Other ethical guidelines concern things such as privacy—can you keep the content of readings you give confidential?

A concern people often have is how to break bad news in a reading. I have read Tarot for over twenty years, and my advice is not to hide that which might be negative, but also try to see further and advise the person how to get through whatever may be difficult. Never give a negative prediction without offering some kind of hope. Also, remind the querent that the future can be changed, that there is always free will.

There are two kinds of meditation: the kind used by more Eastern practices, such as Buddhism, and those that are used by Western magickal practitioners. Each is valid, and each is valuable for our purposes. Eastern meditation tends to focus on "mindfulness"—a practice that promotes calm, peacefulness, and harmony. It also works on emptying the mind of all other thought, which can be difficult in this busy Western world. However difficult it is for us Westerners, this approach to meditation provides the cornerstone for concentration and openness.

Western magick offers the practice of pathworking, guided meditations, or both; I will discuss how to approach both. Both approaches require a quiet place where you can be alone with your practice and not be disturbed. Both require postures in which you will be comfortable but not fall asleep (for example, sitting and not lying down).

For the Eastern practice, spend five minutes each day, building to ten minutes and then to fifteen eventually. Sit comfortably. Rather than closing your eyes, keep your eyes open but your gaze unfocused. In other words, you are not staring, and your surroundings are not important. Breath is important but should not dominate the meditation. Breathing should be soft, like your gaze.

With mindfulness meditation, as thoughts come to you, acknowledge that they are there, but let them go. Do not stay with the thoughts or become swept up in them. In a way, you are emptying the mind.

This process may seem very simple and at the same time can be incredibly difficult for those of us with "busy brains." The key is not to lose hope but to keep working on your meditation practice. This is training your mind to focus, and it is incredibly important if you want to be able to practice magick. Do not give up! Everyone has this ability within themselves; it may just take time for you to develop the skill, since our Western culture is not very supportive of it.

For the Western practice, further exploration is encouraged in the form of pathworkings (journeys along the Tree of Life on the Qabala) and guided meditation. Meditations such as these might begin with something that seems very much like mindfulness meditation, but then move into a specific journey that is read to you, and that your mind then takes. You might have your own interpretations of that journey, but there are specific experiences the writer of the journey is hoping for you to have. These deepen our understanding of the paths on the Tree of Life, and also in exploring things such as the elements, and also gods and goddesses. Some journeys are extremely specific—to the point of being rigid—and some allow for a lot of interpretation. gain, both forms have their value.

Grounding and Centering

This is a term you will hear a lot if you attend rituals of any kind. You will often be encouraged to ground and center before and after ritual, and you may wonder what this means, if you are not familiar with magick in general. Grounding and centering is a very important practice, since it brings you back to reality after workings of all kinds, even those that may not seem very intense.

Why would you even *want* to ground and center and return to reality after experiencing the lovely, light, floating feeling that both ritual and meditation can bring? The reasons are many, not the least of which is we live in *this* world, and we need to reattune ourselves to it. A bad leftover-energy headache is not something anyone enjoys—and it can often happen if you don't ground and center yourself. Not paying attention to one's surroundings may not always be the worst thing that can happen, but sometimes it can be the cause of the worst thing that can happen. Some group leaders are very aware of this and may already have grounding and centering written into their meditations and rituals. If they do not, then it is important for you to know how to do it.

The simplest method of grounding is to simply bend down (if standing) and touch the actual ground you are standing on. Feel your connection to the Earth and allow any excess energy you may be carrying around to flow out of your hands and fingertips and into the ground. The next thing to do may be to eat some food. Also, hugging another person is a very good way to ground, assuming they wish to be hugged, so ask first. You may notice there is a lot of hugging going on after ritual—it is a great way to connect with community and provides the added benefit of bringing yourself back to your body.

A very simple visualization is used by many in the craft for grounding and centering, and I confess that I do not know if this idea originated with an individual or not, but I do know that it is very effective. Stand straight and tall. Visualize yourself as a tree—your trunk is the trunk of a tree. Feel the energy that runs up and down your spinal column as the energy that flows through a tree. Now, feel that your feet, planted firmly on the ground, are the roots of this tree. Feel your roots reaching into the deep earth, taking in all the nourishment that the soil has to offer. Feel that energy rising gently, rising up through your trunk, and now up and out into your arms, which become the branches. The branches of the tree that is you take in the warmth and heat of the sun, and the nurturing of the stars and the moon. Again, feel that energy move back down and mingle with the more earthly energy. Feel yourself stable and solid . . . and you are grounded and centered.

Divination

There are a variety of ways to approach divination. The names for many of them end in "-mancy," from the ancient Greek *manteia* (divination), or "-scopy," from the Greek *skopein* (to look into, to behold).

Trying to determine which method works for you can be a bit dizzying, given the lists one finds on the internet. I would recommend working with things that seem familiar or "call" to you. Many people will find themselves "drawn" to a particular kind of divination, such as Tarot, runes, or astrology. As always, I recommend picking something that works for you, and sticking with it in a consistent manner. Begin and be gentle with yourself. Some people open to information immediately; others need more time. People also receive information in different ways—some auditory, some visually, some through simple feelings. Try not to compare your experience with that of other people.

Developing Your Intuition and Psychic Abilities

There is one thing no one can teach you, and that is how it is that you receive information. Some people actually hear information (clairaudience), some see it (clairvoyance), while others simply sense or feel it (clairsentience). Some people are fortunate enough to receive information in two or more ways. The important thing is that you not judge yourself or compare yourself to how someone else appears to be doing. The only way that you will find out which way you receive information is to practice. In this portion of our discussion, you will be learning some exercises that will help you see how you receive information. The key to success with these exercises is to trust yourself. Do not judge any of the thoughts that come into your head; simply remain open to them. Sometimes you may think that you are making things up or simply pulling up things that are already in your head. Remember that Spirit has to use whatever is inside you in order to communicate. You must be trusting enough to receive the information.

The exercises here must be done with a partner, preferably someone who is like-minded and would also like to explore psychic development. The second key to success with these exercises is that once you trust yourself, you must speak up and share what you see with your partner. More information may come if you allow yourself to speak and give voice to that which comes to you. Your partner must remain silent and not comment while you speak—all sharing should be saved until you are finished. The reason for this is not to interrupt the flow that is coming through while you are working. The final key to success

is PRACTICE. You may not always succeed immediately, but if you keep working at it, you should be able to receive something.

Seeing Auras

The first exercise is to work on seeing auras. At this point in time, the key is not to interpret them, but simply to be able to see them. Everyone has several layers of subtle bodies; sometimes it is easiest to see the first layer. The first step for this exercise is to find a blank wall painted either white or in a neutral color. The room may be lit, but not too harshly. Either you or your partner can start by standing in front of that wall. Relax and make your eyes go "soft"—that is, don't focus too hard on your friend. Take time and look at your friend, and the background of the wall. You should be able to see *something*, some kind of energy, possibly appearing as though it is radiating out from your friend. Don't judge yourself if you don't see anything immediately—it takes time. Switch and see what your friend can see of your aura.

Psychometry

For this exercise, both you and your friend will need an object—small enough to be held—that belongs to each of you. Items that are ideal for psychometry are items such as rings—metal conducts energy well, and rings are very personal. The more personal the item, the better.

You and your friend should be facing one another and decide who will try first. Take the object of the other person in your hand and hold it. Keep your mind clear and open and listen for what may come to you. Again, do not judge the information. As it comes to you, speak it aloud to your partner. Your partner should remain silent for the duration of the exercise. Try this with the object for about five minutes. When the time is up, now is the time for your partner to share whether there was anything accurate in their reading. When you are done, the two of you may switch.

ESP Cards

The last exercise involves the use of ESP cards. There are ESP cards available in all kinds of colors, shapes, and sizes, but the best ones are of the simplest design. You can find a very suitable set of cards here: http://www.mdani.demon.co.uk/para/zener.htm. For our purposes, all you need to do is cut them out and they are ready to use. (If this is something you might be working with a lot, you may want to mount the cards on board and laminate them.) Divide the cards up between you and your partner. Decide who will try first—one of you will be the sender, and the other will be the receiver. The sender pulls a card from his or her pile and holds it so that the receiver cannot see it. Stare at the card and imagine sending the image on it to your partner. Your partner then will state, out loud, which image it is, doing their best to discern what you are sending. Once they state the card out loud, do not comment on if they are right or wrong, but set the card down and move to the next one. Note the number of cards they get right and the number of cards they get wrong. And, of course, switch once you've gotten through the pile.

Conclusion

In conclusion, the best way to approach divination and psychic development is through PRACTICE. If you work with the above exercises as well as putting some kind of meditation into daily practice, you will become more open and more intuitive. Working with systems such as the Tarot and the runes is also helpful and can be done in conjunction with the previous exercises. Most of all, be gentle with yourself and do not be afraid to try again!

CHAPTER TEN

RITUAL CONSTRUCTION

reating your own rituals may seem difficult and awkward at first, but once you get the hang of it, you'll be able to write your very own rituals, using this format and adapting it to your needs. There are books available that have prewritten rituals you may use, and while there is nothing wrong with this, writing rituals of your own design that are tailored exactly to your needs is extremely satisfying and educational. Most Wiccan rituals follow a particular pattern, which is easy to follow. Once you are familiar with the process, you can change or deviate from the pattern in the way that works best for you.

As mentioned, most rituals follow the pattern outlined below. Ultimately, the first step before writing a ritual is deciding what kind of ritual you want to do. Will this be a celebratory ritual? Is it a ritual being done for a magickal working? Be very clear about what you wish to accomplish, and try to keep your intent focused as well. Having too many goals in one ritual can muddy the outcome for all the goals. This is all very important, but before getting into the particulars of deciding how and when and what to write for your ritual, we'll begin by looking at these steps.

I have been to rituals where much time has been spent on casting and calling the quarters—and yes, I devoted an entire chapter to the discussion of cast and call—however, the most important part of the ritual is the goal of the ritual, the "meat" of the ritual, if you will, or what some might call "the working." This is where you want to put the focus: What needs to happen here? Even with a celebratory ritual, there needs to be intent created. You also want to appeal to all parts of the participants' selves—the heart, the mind, the body, the soul, and the spirit. I will elaborate below with how this can be done.

Setup and Preparation of Ritual Space

This entails whatever you need to make the space ready, whatever needs to be on your altar, whatever "props" are needed. Are you creating your own incense for this rite? What color of candles will you be using? If you are inclined toward wearing ritual robes while working, you may wish at this point to get dressed. Anything you need to do to set up the physical part of the ritual goes here. This is also where the more physical needs may be addressed—sights, scents, sounds, touch, even taste, if you are including food in the ritual. All these things go toward making a full sensory experience for participants.

Purification

This can be as simple or elaborate as you like. The idea behind this step is to set aside mundane concerns and prepare to enter the circle. How much you want to be purified depends on how much detail goes into this step. You can go so far as to prepare a ritual bath for yourself, complete with scented bath salts or oils, or it can be as simple as using salt water to sprinkle one's self and using incense prior to entering sacred space. Salt water includes the elements of Water and Earth, and incense includes the elements of Fire and Air.

The number of people present may also make a difference in this step. Purification baths seem to work best for initiations (and only the initiate takes the purification bath, while everyone else gets ready) or for solitary rituals. At large gatherings, we do what we call the "car wash" style of purification. One person stands on either side of the entryway to the circle—one with salt water, the other with either incense or smudge stick. As entrants come through the gate, they are sprinkled lightly with water and smudged with incense.

Another alternative is something called a drum wash. When done properly, this can have a profound effect. It is most effective when there is more than one drummer, preferably with an even number of people who can stand on either side of the opening of the circle. The drummers play a simple rhythm, and participants process between them into the circle. As participants pass through, they can feel the powerful beat of the drums around them, clearing out the energy.

Cast the Circle and Calling the Quarters

This is where the actual ritual begins. Once the circle is cast and the quarters are called, no one should leave the circle unless they "cut" themselves out (or are led out by whatever protocol is being used). There are a number of ways in which this can be accomplished, and a number of patterns followed by various Wiccan groups. The main idea is to cast a circle of energy to keep good energy in and bad energy out. Most Wiccan rituals do not involve invocation of frightening things that must be kept at bay, or things that must be kept out of the circle. For most of us, casting the circle and calling the quarters is about establishing sacred space, regardless of the space we are in.

There are a variety of different castings to be used on other occasions—the most common pattern is the quarters-cast circle. There are also triangle castings, and other configurations, some of which are compatible with a quarters casting and some that are not. Having said this, those castings tend to be for more-advanced workings, and for the purposes of this book, we will stick with the quarters-cast circle.

Many Wiccan circles cast the circle first, by tracing the energy around the circle (around the participants, keeping them IN the circle), starting from the east and then ending in the east. At this point, they would call the quarters. In the Assembly of the Sacred Wheel, the circle is drawn as the quarters are called, essentially tracing the line of energy from quarter to quarter.

Some people never call the quarters; however, in the tradition in which I was trained, the quarters are called (and dismissed at the end) for every ritual. The idea is to have all four of the sacred elements present as well as Spirit, which is present in the circle.

Here are some examples of circle castings:

Circle Casting #1

This is one of the easiest ways to cast a circle and also encourages participants to be aware of one another and each others' energies (we did this in my Brownie troop—little did my Brownie leader know she was contributing to the paganism of a minor!). The person standing in the east begins the circle by squeezing the hand of the person next to her left. They in turn squeeze the hand of the person next to them, and so on, until the squeeze makes its way back to the first person in the east. The circle is cast. This can be done even more formally, with each person stating aloud, "I cast this circle hand to hand," before taking the hand of the person next to them until all are holding hands.

Circle Casting #2

This is the most traditional method used, and the one you will find in most books on Wicca. Beginning in the east, take your athame and trace a line on the ground (not literally—stand and then direct your athame toward the ground), moving to the south, the west, the north, and then back to the east. As you do so, visualize a line of blue flame rising to make a perfect circle. The line of blue flame is important—it is that which will keep the energies of your circle intact.

Calling the Quarters

There are a number of ways in which to call the quarters (please see chapter 11 for a more thorough discussion about calling the quarters). Some groups actually command them to come to their circle, while others simply invite. We are not Enochian magicians or chaos magicians trying to summon demons and other entities to our command. We are Wiccans, so we can invite the elemental energies to join us, and they are always glad to take part.

There are a number of commonly used wordings to invite the quarters, some of which are listed below:

"I summon, stir, and call you up, creatures of the East . . ."
"Hail to the Guardians of the Watchtowers of the East, Powers of Air . . ."

How you choose to call the quarters depends entirely on you. Either you will want to work with quarter calls someone else has written, or you may write your own. As always, writing your own creates your own personal stamp on the ritual, making it more effective for YOU. You will want to familiarize yourself fully with the quarters, and the attributions for each one to see what you wish to incorporate into your calls. Casting the circle, calling the quarters, and establishing sacred space are so important that I have devoted the entire next chapter to the subject.

Once the circle is cast and the quarters are called, it is common for all to come together, holding hands in circle to say, "The circle is cast. We are between the worlds in a time that is not a time and a place that is not a place. We are in sacred space. Blessed be."

Statement of Intent

This is the part of the ritual where you make your intent clear to the gods, to the seen and unseen. For group rituals, this has the benefit of reminding everyone why they are there, and can provide additional insight into the event. For example, if you are celebrating the spring equinox, this can be a good time to tell stories of the mythology of that particular season. Most of all, this is a part of the ritual where you make yourself clear, and in magick it is best to be direct and specific.

The clearer your statement of intent, the more likely you will accomplish whatever your ritual goals may be. If you intend to do a magickal working in sacred space, here is a time where you can declare what you are working toward. Again, you want to be specific. Words have power, and stating what you want is a good way of ensuring that your intent is clear.

Invocation of Deity

It is hoped that by this time, you've given some thought to our prior discussion on patrons and pantheons and have an idea of the gods/goddesses you wish to work with. The deity or deities you invoke can be your own personal patrons, or they may be deities that are appropriate to your purpose; for example, if you are doing a healing ritual, you may wish to call upon a deity of healing. As mentioned in the discussion on patrons and pantheons, try to stick with one pantheon per ritual. Sometimes it is appropriate to call a deity of each gender to the circle, and sometimes you want to call just one. It all depends on what your intent is.

Your invocation may take the form of a specially written chant to call the deities to the circle. At this point in time, we are lucky in that there have been many recordings of excellent chants to be used in ritual, and even websites with chants you can download or listen to. Chanting is always good because it raises energy. However, if singing is not your thing, you may wish to write a spoken invocation. There are many beautiful poetic ways in which to call the gods to ritual.

The most important thing about your invocation is that it is heartfelt, and something that will make the deity in question actually want to be present. I have learned that the more emotion is put into the invocation, it is more likely that deity will show up. Establishing a relationship with the deity being invoked beforehand is also recommended. Why would they want to visit if you've never spoken to them before?

Raising Energy or Consciousness

This is the part of the ritual where energy is raised to help accomplish whatever your stated goal in the Statement of Intent was. One of the things you might read about in books about Wicca is "raising the cone of power." The cone of

power is essentially the energy that is raised by the circle and then sent up and out to accomplish the ritual's stated goals.

Energy can be raised in a variety of ways. Many groups seem to prefer to do it by using chant. Chant is easy and requires no equipment except the human voice, and most chants are easily learned. Choose a chant that you or your group can easily learn and sing—often, simple chants with only a few lines are best. Everyone chants while holding the goal in mind, visualizing the energy building as a cone of power in the center of the circle. Chanting can go on for quite some time as the energy builds, and it is okay to harmonize, change the chant up a little, or vary things so long as the energy continues to build. As with the invocation, the most important thing is the sincerity, and the actual energy of those present chanting. A beautiful voice is lovely, but it is not required. Some groups hold hands, which they will raise slowly, a bit at a time, until everyone's hands are in the center of the circle. When the chanting reaches a peak, the hands and the energy are released.

Another way of raising energy is through drumming. Drumming is like chanting—easy to do, and great for those who prefer not to sing! (Some of us, myself included, can not sing and drum at the same time. I guess this is the magickal equivalent of not being able to walk and chew gum at the same time.) Drumming is a very powerful means of raising energy, as evidenced by books and albums in recent years from people such as Mickey Hart, Gabrielle Roth, and Dead Can Dance.

Ecstatic dance can also be a means of raising energy. I have seen ecstatic dance most often used in combination with drumming or chanting, or other musical instruments in circle. It can be wondrous to see people in a circle, whirling and spinning about, raising the energy.

Guided meditation can be a way to raise energy, but the kind of energy raised is not as powerful as the energy raised through chanting or drumming. One person can lead the group in a visualization in which they "see" the energy building and send it out toward its intended goal. This is a much-quieter way of raising energy—most useful for situations in which one does not want to stir up alarm, such as in an apartment—or for providing healing with a sick person present.

Grounding and Centering

After raising all that energy, it is absolutely necessary to ground and center properly afterward. Yes, raising energy feels great, and sometimes you can get something of a buzz from it. However, energy that is not grounded becomes stale and can cause uncomfortable side effects later. Some people speak of a "third-eye headache." This is almost like a hangover, in that one feels the effects the morning after! If you work to build grounding and centering into your circle, you can circumvent this problem. Sometimes people who are newer to the craft are unaware of the need to ground, and having a moment in the ritual when everyone can do this is a good idea.

Grounding can be done simply in visualizing one's self as a tree, with roots stretching far into the Mother Earth. Some people like to take it a step further and actually touch the earth. Nearly anything physical you can do will help ground you, such as washing your hands or eating, which brings us to the next step . . .

Cakes and Ale

In this part of the ritual, participants partake of food and drink. Apart from the benefit of helping everyone to ground, this also allows members to share a little time with each other in sacred space. Now is the time when participants can share visions they had, or feelings they experienced in ritual.

The cakes and ale themselves are kept fairly simple. They may be reflective of the season; for example, particular spices or herbs might be used that go with the holiday—it just requires a little research. Sometimes alcohol might be used for the ale—it could be mead or wine—or not, depending on the needs of the group.

The cakes and ale are blessed prior to sharing, and in our tradition we pass them around the circle to one another, saying, "May you never hunger," as we pass the food to the next person, and "May you never thirst," as we pass the ale to the next person. One of the ways in which we celebrate cakes and ale is with the performance of the Symbolic Great Rite, mentioned in chapter 3. Do be careful that this portion of the ritual does not get too out of hand or go on for too long. Energy can dissipate if there is too much joking and sharing before you are ready to dismiss the circle and officially end the ritual. Keep it simple.

Dismissal

This is the part of the ritual where any deities invoked are thanked for their presence, and the quarters are thanked and dismissed. It is important to dismiss the circle for much the same reason that it is a good idea to ground and center. An undismissed circle can create stale energy, and although most of the energies associated with Wicca are fairly mild, you really do not want stale energy hanging around, because it may attract unwanted spirits.

Dismissal can be as simple or elaborate as needed. Some people simply go to each quarter and say, "Hail and farewell," while others use dismissals with more detail. Once the circle has ended, nearly every magickal group I have encountered says, "The circle is open, but unbroken, merry meet, merry part, and merry meet again!"

The Fine Art of Crafting Ritual Intent

So . . . what will your ritual be all about? Being certain of this is the most important part of crafting rituals. As always, keep your intent focused and keep it simple. Trying to have too many goals in one ritual will muddy the energy, and nothing will be accomplished. If you want to do a ritual for psychic insight, then that should be your sole focus. Work on gathering information that will be specific to your intent. For example, if you are doing a rite of healing (as mentioned earlier), call upon deities specific to healing. As always, work with deities within the same pantheon who are compatible with one another. When you write your quarter calls, you can ask for the kinds of healing energies each element might provide. If you are doing a ritual for a particular holiday, research what kinds of myths you may wish to enact within the ritual space. In some cases, the energy for a ritual might be raised during the enactment of a myth (for example, if Persephone is coming out of the Underworld for a spring equinox ritual, you could chant songs to welcome her back).

As with all things magickal, practice is the key to learning. Often in Wicca, learning to write good ritual is a trial-and-error process. We often learn what doesn't work by what falls flat in the rituals we have written. The key is not to let it get you down, but to learn from mistakes and keep trying. There is nothing more satisfying then celebrating ritual with good friends and coven mates!

CHAPTER ELEVEN

CASTING THE CIRCLE AND CALLING THE QUARTERS

An Important Skill

The casting of a circle is an acknowledgement of the limits of human consciousness and is a tool to reach beyond those limits by choosing specific boundaries and limits. —Domínguez, *Casting Sacred Space*, p. 9

hen witches do ritual, they create sacred space in whatever space they are in, whether that space happens to be outdoors, in a dedicated temple space, or in someone's living room. One of the most vital ways in which Wiccans create sacred space is by casting a circle and calling the quarters.

Why Is It Important to Cast the Circle and Call the Quarters?

If the circle is a microcosm of the entire universe, then the quarters-cast circle serves to scale the universe down to human consciousness. In other traditions, the circle and quarters are often seen as a boundary with guardians (the lare or watchtowers) to ensure nothing unseemly enters the sacred space. Ceremonial magicians are often calling on entities that could be quite dangerous and need to be hemmed in by the circle. In Wicca, we are usually creating sacred space, not trying to contain demons or other entities. Having said that, however, it is important to create a circle as a field of protection from anything unseemly on the outside.

Many traditions beyond Wicca call upon and acknowledge the four sacred directions, including the Celts, Native American, Kongo (African), Buddhist, Christian (the archangels), Egyptian (four sons of Horus and four protectress goddesses of the Nile), Greek (the four winds Eurus, Notus, Zephyrus, and Boreas), Hindu (the tattvas), Japanese (Shinto), and Judaic. It is interesting for experimentation's sake to try using some of these other systems, which you might like to do at some point. Once you decide which way works best for you, I highly suggest you use that pattern for most of your rituals. Consistency establishes a pattern, which has more power than being overly eclectic and trying many different ways every time.

Calling the quarters plots a specific coordinate in space and time: we are between the worlds, in all of the worlds, and in no worlds—all at once; a place that is not a place and a time that is not a time.

The most important thing to bear in mind about casting and calling is that YOU are the most important tool. We use an athame or a wand to direct the energy, but ultimately, you are the most important component. It is the ability of the person who is doing the casting to direct the energy that is the most important tool. Sometimes tools are necessary, but ultimately, a circle may be cast and the quarters called, using the energy of a human being or human beings alone.

As with all effective magickal workings, self-development and self-actualization are the most-important tools. Your ability to focus and concentrate are your best tools. Having said that, do not be trapped into thinking you must be PERFECT. We are human beings, after all, and sometimes may flub a pronunciation, or mix up north with south and so on. The best thing to do in such a situation is to calm your mind and simply begin again. Beating yourself over the head for "messing up" leads nowhere.

Preparation for Casting and Calling

The following questions are important in determining how you will create a casting.

What is this ritual FOR? Choose or create your casting from the ritual's intent.

Is the ritual celebratory for a particular season?

Is the ritual a magickal working? An initiation? A spell?

Do the research needed if necessary.

There are example quarter calls at the end of this chapter—I recommend trying those out to see how they feel to you. If you like, you may want to practice calling the quarters by using those calls. If you don't like them, by all means work on writing your own. Use the information on each element that we covered in chapter 4 to guide you on key words to include in your calls.

Once you have determined the kind of casting you will do, keep a calm, clear focus. Memorize the wording you will use if necessary. I find this helps a great deal, although "cheat sheets" are fine if you need to remind yourself of key words. Visualization is also very helpful: Are there symbols you can use during the calls to assist the casting? Symbols such as the tattvas can be very helpful.

Once you have done all of the above, and the time for the ritual has come, enter the circle quietly, before it is cast. Go to each quarter and quietly meditate and connect with each quarter beforehand.

During purification, remind yourself that you are entering the circle in perfect love and perfect trust. This is always your goal. What do you need to do for yourself to ensure perfect love and perfect trust? Above all, put aside mundane worries and concerns.

During Casting and Calling

Now is the time to put aside self-judgment. Silence the critical committee that lives in your head, and do not beat yourself up if you make a mistake, or worry ahead of time if you will make a mistake. Magick requires a level of comfort with vulnerability.

Ground and center first. Usually when we are doing ritual as a group, the high priestess will lead a grounding-and-centering meditation so everyone will be in the right frame of mind when we enter the circle. You can do it for yourself when you are on your own.

Some groups like to decorate their quarters with full altars composed of objects that relate to that quarter, and some like a simple candle of the corresponding quarter lit to mark the quarter. It is entirely up to you what you need to feel as though you are making the quarters welcome. It is also appropriate to decorate each quarter according to the holiday being celebrated, or whatever purpose is bringing you to ritual.

While casting, you need to be open to sensing energy. Become aware of the way you receive information: Is it visual? Auditory? Some other sense? You want both to be aware of and to direct the energy. When we cast the circle and call the quarters as a group, the group energy also helps to direct the energy. Some people become worried that the energy is being directed at them—in a way it is, but that energy is there for you to then direct it toward calling the quarters.

How to Do It in Real Life!

In the tradition in which I was trained, we always move clockwise, sunwise, or deosil in the circle, even at the end, when taking the circle down. You may have noticed in other traditions that they go widdershins (counterclockwise) when banishing. The intent in moving sunwise is to leave some magick behind.

Go to wherever east is represented within your circle. With your athame or wand, trace the outline of a circle around the people who are standing in the circle. You can direct the energy by stretching your arm out, and you may trace the circle either on the ground or in the air. If you are trying to keep a large amount of space in the circle, you may wish to visualize a circle forming beyond the confines of the individuals standing in it. Walk all the way around until you come back to the east. At that point, you will be ready to cast the quarters.

Begin once again in the east. You will recite your casting and then open the quarter gate by drawing an invoking pentacle in the air with your athame or wand. Your calling may be as simple as "Spirits of the east, I call you forth to join this circle," or as complex as the calls at the end of this chapter.

As you call, if you are able, it helps to have a symbol you have visualized to aid the casting. You can also visualize gates opening, and the beings associated with that quarter entering the circle. Once you have drawn your invoking pentacle, this is the time to announce, "The gates of the east are open," and then, "Hail and welcome," which everyone will repeat (or "Blessed be," or whatever form of acknowledgment you have chosen).

And now, walk to the southern quarter, moving clockwise. en you come to the south, once again you will stop and recite your call. You will move then to the west, and then to the north. When you finish with the north, complete the circle by visualizing the line of blue flame connecting back to the east.

Once the circle is complete, step back into the circle, where everyone will join hands. Announce, "The circle is cast," and whatever wording you wish— usually it has to do with being between the worlds, for instance.

Do note that some traditions have different approaches. Some people begin by calling the quarters in the north. As I mentioned once before, some folks change the attributions they use for the directions. Some people move north to south or east to west since they want to emphasize the equal-armed cross pattern. So long as one remains consistent with the tradition they are working with, it really is immaterial. I am presenting you with the way that I have been trained to do it, which is consistent with many traditions.

As with all magick, anytime you call something up, you want to send it back home. Generally, we will not be calling up anything frightening or fierce, but a circle that is not taken down after a ritual leaves behind stale energy. It just doesn't feel very good. We always dismiss the quarters after ritual, following a pattern similar to the one used for calling them. The wording does not need to be elaborate, unless you've called something out of the quarter that may require special acknowledgment.

To dismiss, once again move to the east and recite your dismissal. A typical one might say, "Spirit of the East, we thank you for your presence. We bid you now to depart to your lovely realms." Then draw a banishing pentacle and announce, "The Gates of the East are closed. Hail and farewell." And everyone will repeat, "Hail and farewell."

You would then move to the south and so on, until you are back at the east. Once there, you may announce, "The circle is open, but unbroken . . . etc."

And let the feasting begin!

Some Sample Quarter Calls

Helena's Poetic Quarter Calls

Spirits of the East
Gossamer Sylphs sing your crystalline songs
Open our minds to magick and possibility
Bring with you the breath of She
Who opens the Infinite
And may She inspire us
With the Gifts of Air.

Spirits of the South
Jewel Red Salamanders come forth from the glowing embers
Awaken our passions, stir our souls
Bring with you the desire of She
Who is all Desire
And may She inspire us
With the Gifts of Fire.

Spirits of the West
Glorious, beautiful Undines
The call of our hearts invites you in
The dreamers would awaken to the oceans of the infinite
Bring with you the love of She
Who is Love unto all living things
And may She inspire us
With the Gifts of Water

Spirits of the North
Might Gnomes who dwell within the deeps
We invite you forth with the jewels of creation
Help us to see the foundations of All
Bring with you the Wisdom of She
Who is Infinite Understanding
And May She inspire us
With the Gifts of Earth

Quarter Calls Created for Samhain

East:
Guardians of the Watchtowers of the East, Spirits of Air!
Spirits of Intellect, Reason, Inspiration!
Help us to be clear of mind and open to messages of our ancestors in this
ritual.
Please join us on this night as we honor our beloved dead.
Guardians of the East, the gates are open!
Hail and welcome!

South:
Guardians of the Watchtowers of the South, Spirits of Fire!
Spirits of Passion, Drive, and Energy!
Help us to feel the energy of our ancestors in this ritual.
Please join us on this night as we honor our beloved dead.
Guardians of the South, the gates are open!
Hail and welcome!

West:
Guardians of the Watchtowers of the West, Spirits of Water!
Spirits of Emotion, Love, and Intuition!
Help us to feel the connections of our ancestors in this ritual.
Please join us on this night as we honor our beloved dead.
Guardians of the West, the gates are open!
Hail and welcome!

North:
Guardians of the Watchtowers of the North, Spirits of Earth!
Spirits of Stability, Strength, and Wisdom!
Help us to know the strength and wisdom of our ancestors in this ritual.
Please join us tonight as we honor our beloved dead.
Guardians of the North, the gates are open!
Hail and welcome!

Exercise

In the chapter on the tools and elements, we talked about the attributes of each element, and I hope you also did the guided meditations for each quarter. In order to more easily develop your own quarter calls, and to understand their meanings more fully, we will now do some writing prompts. Give yourself fifteen minutes for each and just free-write; don't judge what is coming into your head. When you have done all four prompts, read the directions that follow the prompts.

Writing Prompt 1:

When I think of the element of Air, I think of

_____.

Writing Prompt 2:

When I think of the element of Fire, I think of

_____.

Writing Prompt 3:

When I think of the element of Water, I think of

_____.

Writing Prompt 4:

When I think of the element of Earth, I think of

_____.

After the Writing:

Now take a look at what you have written. Find key words that really reflect what you feel about each quarter and element. See now if you can craft your own quarter calls based on these key words. The phrasing of each call should be consistent, as you see in the examples given in this chapter. Whatever you do in one quarter, you should do for all of them—in other words, if you call in the elemental ruler of one quarter, you should call in the elemental ruler for all the other elements. If you call on the elemental being of one quarter, you should call in the elemental being of all four quarters. Magick works best when it is consistent.

When you have finished writing, take time and now try out using your calls to call the quarters into the circle, taking note of how the energy feels at each quarter. Note anything you feel is significant in your journal. In time, you will want to have a lot of practice both with calling the elements and quarters into the circle, AND be able to write specific quarter calls for specific purposes. As always, YOUR INTENT is the most important part of any magickal operation.

CHAPTER TWELVE

SPELL CRAFTING

 Spell work is something that many Wiccans do—after all, don't witches cast spells? Isn't that what we're supposed to do? Spell-casting is, of course, a choice, but many people consider it a definite part of and a perk to being Wiccan. Spell-casting can be a way of exerting control over one's life, and can be extremely empowering. There are many approaches to spell work, and an infinite amount of possibilities in approach and execution. Although there are many books on prewritten spells, to my mind there is nothing quite so satisfying as writing something yourself, tailor made to your own needs. Something you have crafted yourself, and in which you have invested your own time and energy, can be much more successful, depending on your needs, than something found in a book.

Working with spells others have written can be quite effective, depending on the spell and your need at the time. A Google search for spells on the internet will yield a number of spells that are tried and true and have worked for large numbers of people. One might wonder why this is so. As I have mentioned elsewhere, pathways that are well carved out on the astral and that have been traveled before always have a way of working more quickly. Whether or not you write your own spells, there are a few things to keep in mind.

Just like with writing rituals, when doing spell workings, your intent must be clear and well crafted. Just like writing rituals, the first step for spell-crafting is to craft your intent. Think it through carefully: What do you want? Why do you want it? As you are thinking about it, also be aware of ethics—will your desires get in the way of someone else's will? We're Wiccan; the rede always applies. Another thing to determine is if you really feel you need to do magick around your desires. You also want to consider at the very least doing the real-world work to back up your magickal efforts—if you are doing magick to find a job, then make sure you are actually also SEEKING one. The goddess will not drop an employer on your doorstep.

Love spells are an area that can be especially tricky. Doing a love spell on a particular person is never a good thing—it interferes with that individual's will (one might also abide by the caveat "Be careful of what you ask for; you may get it"). Instead of aiming for a particular individual, you might try writing down a list of all the qualities you would seek in the ideal partner, and organize your spell around attracting *that kind* of individual you wish to attract. I have always found that love spells also work much better when not trying to go for a particular person—that pesky free-will thing just gets in the way.

I have my own methods for doing spell work, and I can share with you a few things that have worked for me over the years. You may have any number of tools and supplies on hand, but the number one ingredient to any spell is YOU: you and your intent. The more emotionally charged your need is, the more powerful the spell can be—as long as you are not causing harm to anyone else and bringing it back upon yourself. Positive attracts positive, and negative always seems to attract negativity multiplied.

So . . .

Number one: YOU

Number two: Your desired outcome. Keep it simple, keep it straightforward. Do not do one spell to cure all ills; a spell for healing is just for that, not to also bring a new car or new love into your life.

Number three: Stuff. What kind of stuff? Well, tools.

Deciding what tools to use may involve thinking about the kinds of colors associated with what it is you are trying to achieve. Money spells would utilize green. Love spells use red or pink. There are many correspondence charts available to help you determine the kinds of tools you can use to assist you. If you wish to use Tarot cards, you might want to lay out the cards in the perfect reading with the perfect outcome you desire for your spell. Numbers have meaning, so you may wish to incorporate numbers into your spell via the number of candles used, the number of days you light a candle, etc.

Many people also like to consider the time in which they are doing a spell. There are a number of correspondence charts that discuss the significance of each day magickally—which god/goddess rules that day, which hour of the day is ruled by which planet, and so on. If this seems too complicated, you may prefer to consider the phase of the moon—waxing or waning, or full. If the moon is waxing, it is a good time to ask for blessings, prosperity, or an increase in whatever you desire. If the moon is waning, it is a good time for banishing. If you are looking for a job and the moon happens to be waxing, then do a spell to banish poverty. Be creative; there is no end to ways to work with magick.

If you are astrologically inclined, you may want to purchase an ephemeris or a yearly astrological calendar so that you can be informed of planetary alignments throughout the year. Astrology can be very beneficial to doing spell work and magick in general. Using astrological/planetary glyphs can also be part of your spell work. Glyphs can be drawn on all kinds of objects—candles, stones, etc.

Once again, because we are Wiccan, casting spells is different from what might happen in the case of a nonspiritual individual trying to accomplish their goals. Some paths do not attach spiritual significance to doing spell work—if you believe it will work, it will work, so the belief goes. However, our spirituality works for us, not against us. We can ask for a little help from our friends—our patron gods and goddesses. You may even wish to establish an affinity with a particular god or goddess for a particular purpose. If you are asking them for something, then you should certainly pay some attention to them and find out information about them and establish a relationship before asking. As part of the spell-casting process, you can do ritual and ask for your desires formally in circle.

Another completely different approach is one in which you are not using tools at all, but speaking your spell into being. Marion Weinstein speaks of crafting "words of power" in order to achieve one's goals. Her book *Positive Magic* (Weinstein 1994) was one of the first books I ever read about witchcraft and magic, and I still go by her guidelines to this day. A spoken spell is something you can speak aloud in ritual, alone, or in the presence of a group. *Positive Magic* provides an excellent framework for crafting a spoken spell. You can also combine spoken spells with creating a talisman, amulet, or "mojo bag," or candle magick, Tarot cards, etc., depending on what your needs are.

I especially like Marion Weinstein's approach, which takes a variety of factors into account, including free will and nonmanipulation of other people. She lays out the following principles for creating words of power in her book *Positive Magic*:

1. For the Good of All: To truly be positive practitioners of magic, all magick we practice must be for the good of all. No suffering on anyone's part need be involved. Remember that the Charge of the Goddess states, "Nor do I ask for sacrifice."

2. The Universe as Macrocosm: The universe is seen as the source of all life, and we are part of it. We can all tap into the power inherent in the universe as members of the universe.

3. The Microcosm: This is each of us—we all are manifestations of the power of the universe. The old Hermetic axiom holds true: As above, so below. We are each God, We are each Goddess.

4. The Law of Cause and Effect: Words of power are the CAUSE, and the results of those words of power are the EFFECT. We are working with the unseen realm to create the cause, and the effect manifests in the physical realm, or world of form.

5. Free Will: By stating "For the Free Will of All" in your working, you are eliminating the possibility of your work being manipulative.

6. Infinity: The concept of nonlimitation. So many of us operate believing in a kind of poverty principle—there is not enough to go around. This goes against the universe, which is infinite and wants to give us what we ask for. When you include the principle of infinity in your words of power, you are also leaving room for possibilities you may not have even thought of yet.

7. The Concept of Form and Essence: You may not yet be able to specify exactly what you want, but you know the feeling of what you want. This feeling is the key—you state what the essence of what you are working is, and the universe will pick the very best form. As Weinstein says, "Be open to the flexibility of form—not for compromise, but for fulfillment."

8. Transformation: What is magic for if not transformation? Words of power enable us to change our perceptions and ways of thinking—when we are able to do that, we are able to create change in our lives.

9. Love: The universe loves us so much that it wants to give us what we ask for. We also need to remember self-love—we are part of that universe and need to remember our right to respect, love, and nurture ourselves. When we are able to do this, we are able to share love more freely.

10. The Now: Occult work must be done in the present tense: the eternals do not have the same concept of time as we humans. All time is happening now, but for humans it is linear. Always work on thinking in the present tense when doing magic.

There are a variety of variations you might follow. For example, you might wish to acknowledge your own patrons. Weinstein recommends doing this in step 1, stating, "There is One Power, which is Isis and Osiris, and which is perfect fulfillment." You might wish to add qualifiers, such as "with perfect ease" or "with perfect timing," to your statement. Once you have your statement completed, you may proceed with whatever steps you wish to take—chanting over stones/candles to empower them with your spell, carving runes into your candles to embed your intent in them, etc.

Here are some different examples of spells I have created myself or created with the help of friends.

I was fearing for my employment at the university where I work. Things were unstable and budgets were being cut. I didn't want my salary to be cut, but I also didn't want anyone to lose a job because I was keeping mine. I took my contract from the previous semester, which had been signed by several university officials, and placed it in a special bag. I found two blue stones. Blue corresponds to the sphere of Chesed in the Qabala, and also to the concept of MERCY. I visualized my continued employment, lots of students filling my classes, and lots of other faculty and students roaming the campus. I inscribed the stones with the glyph for Jupiter—the planet of plenty—essentially asking the gods to ensure that there would be an abundance of money to go around and that all of us would keep our jobs and prosper. I was in my fourth year of teaching when I did that spell, and I now have tenure, so I believe all is well.

Here's a spell for dealing with some difficult neighbors.
I was living in a neighborhood with lots of unruly although mostly harmless children. They were a bit snotty and had parents who didn't pay attention to them. My rearview mirror had been knocked off my car in an accident, and before I could afford to have it repaired, I was duct-taping it onto my car. Every day, I'd go out to the car and find the kids had torn off the duct tape. The next time I duct-taped my mirror, I inscribed the glyph for Saturn (a planet having to do with restriction and restraint) onto the tape in clove oil. When I next came out to my car, I found that the kids had tried to undo the tape but had failed.

In creating a spell for yourself, I recommend to first meditate on your purpose. Be as clear and specific as possible. Janet and Stewart Farrar tell a story of casting a spell asking for money, and waking up the next day to find Monopoly money strewn across their front lawn. Be specific about how you wish to receive money—what kind of currency! Once you have your purpose in mind, decide how you feel it is best to proceed. Do you want to create an amulet? Use candles of a specific color for your purpose? Do you want to use a specific stone or crystal and charge it with your purpose and then carry it on your person until your goal is achieved?

CHAPTER THIRTEEN

TO COVEN OR NOT TO COVEN

here are many ways of going about being a witch in this wide world of ours, and many people choose to do so by going the solitary route—that is, they practice alone and more or less keep to themselves, perhaps just occasionally entering the larger community of witches. Although being alone can be fulfilling, having a group to work with can provide many rewards, including enjoying the fellowship and friendship that comes from working with a group of like-minded others.

I have rarely spent much of my time as "a witch alone"; however, I have enough experience to speak to a few of the pros and cons of doing so. Being a solitary witch is a choice many witches make, sometimes because they do not have the option of living in an area where there are many like-minded people, or because they do prefer to work alone. Both solitary and group work are valid choices, and I trust you, dear reader, to know yourself and which way you prefer to work.

Being solitary means being completely autonomous and answerable to no one. One of the most appealing things about Wicca is that you can choose to work as you please because there is no central, hierarchical umbrella group overseeing all the other groups, although there are some who have tried to fulfill that role in a variety of ways. You dictate when and where you practice, and how. You can dive deep into any subject, without worrying about whether or not you are going against the grain of your group.

On the other hand, when one works alone, there is no one else with whom you can bounce off ideas, no one to provide feedback on how a ritual or working might feel. It is entirely possible for a witch working alone to summon a great deal of power; however, in my experience, working with a group enhances that potential greatly. I imagine you can see where my particular bias is! Having said that, I do realize that there are as many ways to be a witch as there are people who are witches, and as I said earlier, know yourself.

So what is a coven, exactly? The word "coven" itself is an older word that can sometimes conjure up lewd images of naked women circling around a fire, making pledges to the devil, and sacrificing babies, lamb, and goats. Francisco Goya, Ricardo Falero, and Albrecht Durer made some particularly lurid images of this kind; however, the modern reality is quite different. Witches often spend a lot of time trying to convey what they aren't rather than what they are, and that is not my intent here.

Nowadays, a coven is a group of people who gather together to celebrate an Earth spirituality path that honors holidays and traditions that celebrate the coming and going of the seasons. We also do like the moon and honor the phases of the moon, often meeting at the full moon and new moon, depending on interests and needs. Most covens celebrate pre-Christian deities, often of Europe, but also of Egypt, the Near East, and other areas, again depending on interests and needs.

It should be noted that sometimes people will use other words instead of coven, such as grove, circle, den, cove, clan, tribe, and other names that they may come up with to describe their group. Sometimes people shy away from such words as coven and witch for fear of being isolated from friends, family, and coworkers. It depends on what people are comfortable with. Depending on where you live, and what your life circumstances are, that fear can be very real. Others just prefer to be out in the open, or to call their group a coven and do so in secret.

How many people may belong to a coven? That number can vary, again depending on personal preferences. The traditional number that most people often cite is thirteen, and that number has a number of connotations behind it. For most, any meeting of three or more is considered a number. I personally have found that going above the number thirteen tends to get unwieldy, depending on how much space someone has in which to gather. Some covens host events that outsiders may attend—these are often known as "open rituals," while others are closed, and still others are completely secretive, depending on their tradition.

A tradition is generally a group of covens that all have the same root from the founding coven. The best known of these is the Gardnerian tradition, which can be quite secretive, and whose covens pride themselves on being able to trace their lineage from initiator to initiator all the way back to Gerald Gardner, the founder of that tradition (there will be more on what initiation is in the next paragraph). Several other well-known traditions are the Alexandrian tradition, the Georgian tradition, the Black Forest clan, the Assembly of the Sacred Wheel, Reclaiming, the Blue Star tradition, and Stone Circle Wicca. Traditions that are Dianic are usually limited to women only, although I have heard that is not always the case. The Minoan tradition follows a Hellenic path. The ways in which these traditions work all vary from one another, but their covens follow whatever patterns those traditions have set down in regard to ritual, creating new covens, teaching, practices, approaches to deity, etc.

Training and initiation are parts of belonging to a coven. Members are taught tenets of Wicca, such as the significance of the various holidays, the elements, and various deities, as well as skills such as creating ritual and doing spells, and such things as Tarot, astrology, runes, and qabala, depending on the kinds of things coven leadership is able to offer. Initiation is an important rite of passage for some groups, while in other, less hierarchic covens, it may not matter at all. Initiation usually is the acknowledgment of having gained a specific skill set or having taken on leadership responsibilities and may be part of a coven's hierarchy. For example, in most Gardnerian Wicca, there are three degrees, the third degree being the degree at which one can become a high priest or high Priestess and can then create their own coven.

The ways in which covens are led can also vary greatly from tradition to tradition. In some covens, it is always the high priestess who has the final word. Sometimes it is both high priest and high priestess. Still others are much more egalitarian, even if there are a high priestess and high priest in place as leaders. In the Reclaiming tradition, which was begun by Starhawk, all of its decisions are made through reaching consensus.

In addition to the traditions mentioned above, there are covens that form on their own, without input from a tradition. It may be that people could not find teachers in their region and thus formed a coven in order to learn from and train one another. In these days of the internet, there do seem to be many more avenues of finding groups to work with, and teachers to learn from. It all depends on personal preference and needs.

In terms of ritual, how a group does ritual will vary greatly as well. One thing that you may want to know is whether or not a group practices skyclad. In Gardnerian Wicca, this is a common practice—rituals are performed with the members in the nude. Many believe this is because Gerald Gardner was a naturist. However, many groups do not practice skyclad, but you may want to ask before attending a ritual if they do. Additionally, some groups find wearing ritual garments very important, whereas others are fine with members wearing street clothes. Some covens may have a particular robe they wish members to wear, whereas others don't care as long as you have some articles of clothing you reserve for ritual only.

So, how will you know if belonging to a coven is for you? There are a number of things you may want to consider. Do you like working with groups? Is fellowship of like-minded people important to you? Is learning with a group something you want? What kinds of classes and workshops are you interested in? Can you make the time commitments that a particular group will have (and this varies depending on the group as well)?

If you are fortunate enough to live in an area where there are many groups, it is a great idea to visit those groups and attend their open events so that you can see if you mesh with them, and vice versa. Different groups may also require different things of their members, so take care to find out what those are before making any commitments. Additionally, if people are not willing to take the time to answer your questions or seem cagey about discussing how they do things, they are probably not the best group to join. If you are completely new to Wicca and the notion of covens, try attending a pagan festival or conference if there is one in your area. A large number of people from many traditions tend to be at these events, and you can get a good idea of what you like or don't like.

Now that I've spoken about some of the positive benefits of belonging to a coven, here are a few things to watch out for or, at the very least, to think about. My friend Courtney Weber Hoover recently wrote a wonderful blog post with some great caveats, some of which I will note here. She wrote in her blog post dated September 18, 2019, "5 Reasons to NOT Join a Coven (or Other Magickal Group)," that it is unhealthy to assume that your new coven will become your new family, for a variety of reasons. She wrote, "The goal of the healthy Coven should be to see individuals thrive on their path, which can mean not being expected to bond with every member, and feeling free to leave it when it's time" (Weber 2019, paragraph 5). She also points out that the coven is not a substitute for therapy. Although there are some places these days where pagans can seek clergical pastoral-counseling certificates, more often than not, your high priest or high priestess will not have these credentials, and it is not fair to them or to other coveners to expect therapy from them. If your high priest or high priestess DO have those credentials, then make an appointment and see them professionally. The coven is not a place for group therapy.

It should go without saying, but the coven is also not the place to look for potential dates or to get laid. Sadly, I have seen people approach magickal groups and covens with this very attitude more times than I care to admit. In my experience, sex—even casual sex—can complicate relationships and destroy the good feelings of coveners toward one another. Magick is deep and complicated, and so are relationships. Sex is an exchange of energy, regardless of the conditions under which it occurs. It is true that we often meet people we think we might like romantically in our places of worship, but be very careful of people and groups who seem to be focused on this.

How can you know for sure if a particular group or coven is right for you? The truth is, there are some things about any group that you will not discover until you are a part of that group—and the same is also true of that group's experience of you. There are ways to discern if a coven or circle or grove is the right place for you. Talking to and getting to know the members is key, of course. Make sure you show up to as many of their events as you can before deciding if you will join. Talk to people while you are there. Find out if you have mutual interests both within and without the scope of the group.

Another good question to ask is how long has this group been around? If they have been around for a long time, that is often a good sign. Having said that, longevity is no guarantee that this is a great group for you. Try to talk to both present and former members. Why are current members still participating? Why did former members leave the organization? The answers may help you decide if this is where you want to be. If there are magickal shops or meet-ups in your area, talk to nonmembers and see what they think of the group, if they have any experience of it. Your potential new coven may ask you for references if you have come from another group. Seeking out references from people within and without the group about the group for yourself is absolutely understandable. Any group that seems secretive or cagey about revealing why previous members have left should send up red flags.

This is just a very small look at what covens do, and truly the best way to find out what a coven does is to begin networking and talking to other Wiccans. Before the internet, it was very difficult for us to find one another. Nowadays, one can join a meet-up, find a group online, and find people to meet in person. Regardless of whether you wish to join a coven or not, I do recommend seeking the friendship of other Wiccans for support. Having a community is tremendously important in these troubled times.

Bibliography

Adler, Margot. *Drawing Down the Moon: Witches, Druids, Goddess Worshippers and Other Pagans in America.* New York: Viking, 1970. Republished by Penguin Books, 2006.

Buckland, Raymond. *Buckland's Complete Book of Witchcraft.* Woodbury, MN: Llewellyn, 2012.

Domínguez, Ivo, Jr. *Casting Sacred Space: The Core of All Magickal Work.* Newburyport, MA: Red Wheel Weiser, 2012.

Farrar, Janet, and Stewart Farrar. *A Witches' Bible.* Custer, WA: Phoenix, 1996.

Hutton, Ronald. *The Triumph of the Moon: A History of Modern Pagan Witchcraft.* Oxford: Oxford University Press, 1999.

Kelly, Aidan. *Crafting the Art of Magic.* St. Paul, MN: Llewellyn, 1991.

Starhawk. *The Spiral Dance: A Rebirth of the Ancient Religion of the Great Goddess.* San Francisco: Harper & Row, 1979.

Valiente, Doreen. *The Rebirth of Witchcraft.* Custer, Washington, Phoenix Press. 1989.

Weber, Courtney. "5 Reasons to NOT Join a Coven (or Other Magickal Group)." *Double, Toil and Resist,* September 18, 2019. www.patheos.com/blogs/double-toilandresist/2019/09/5-reasons-to-not-join-a-coven/.

Weinstein, Marion. *Positive Magic: Occult Self-Help.* Atlantic Beach, NY: Earth Magic, 1994.

Useful Wiccan Websites

My Website, of course: https://illuminatedmagick.com

Alchemy Works: A source for herbs, oils, incense, and seeds
https://www.alchemy-works.com/

The Assembly of the Sacred Wheel: https://sacredwheel.org

Azure Green: The Go-To place for all things Witchy and Pagan
https://www.azuregreen.net/

Canes Enable:

These folks are not necessarily Pagan, but they sell beautifully handcrafted besoms as well as umbrellas, canes, walking sticks, shillelaghs, and the like http://www.canes-enable.com

Circle Sanctuary: https://circlesanctuary.org

Coventry Creations: A great source for candles: https://www.somaluna.com/candles/

The Druid's Garden https://druidgarden.wordpress.com/

Holy Clothing: Awesome clothes for ritual garb https://www.holyclothing.com

Incense Warehouse: They have LOTS of incense of all kinds https://www.incensewarehouse.com/

Magickal Omaha: This is a bricks and mortar store from whom I have ordered all kinds of things from their online shop. They are super helpful! https://www.magicalomaha.com/

Mandragora Magicka – a national networking site to help you locate groups, shops, and others in your area of the United States https://www.mandragora-magika.com/

Sacred Source: Statues, Sculptures of Gods, Goddesses, and other esoteric beings https://sacredsource.com

Sacred Texts: The Internet's Largest Resource of sacred texts from all over the world, from ancient to modern https://www.sacred-texts.com/

Great source for candles of all kinds: https://www.somaluna.com/candles/

Silver Ravenwolf's Website: https://silverravenwolf.wordpress.com/

Stone Circle Wicca: https://stonecirclewicca.org

Thorn Mooney's Website: https://thornthewitch.wordpress.com

The Troth: https://thetroth.org

The Wild Hunt: Modern Pagan News and Perspectives: https://wildhunt.org

Useful Wiccan Books

Casting Sacred Space, Ivo Dominguez, Jr.: How to create sacred space for a variety of purposes in a variety of ways. Very useful.

Cunningham's Book of Incense, Oils, and Brews, Scott Cunningham: Another great treasure trove from Scott Cunningham on creating your own incense, oils, and brews.

Cunningham's Book of Magical Herbs, Scott Cunningham: A great treasure trove on herbs and their uses.

Drawing Down the Moon, Margot Adler: A great look at Witches, Wiccans, and Neo-Pagans of all stripes in the United States.

The Heart of Wicca, Ellen Cannon Reed: A very readable introduction to what is meant by Wicca being a mystery tradition.

Keys to Perception, Ivo Dominguez, Jr.: A great book with a myriad of ways to develop your psychic abilities.

The Master Book of Herbalism, Paul Beyerl: This was and to me still is the benchmark for the magickal and mundane uses of herbs.

Practical Astrology for Witches and Pagans, Ivo Dominguez, Jr.: Scheduling can be everything - and astrology can be overwhelming for beginners. Ivo breaks it down so that you can plan the best dates and times for all of your magickal operations.

Psychic Witch, Matt Auryn: Matt's approach to Witchcraft and honing your talents is relatable and highly useful.

Spiral Dance, StarHawk: This is one of the first books I ever read on Wicca, and the work still profoundly influences me to this day.

Strategic Sorcery, Jason Miller: Jason doesn't consider himself a Witch, but he is a great magician and this book is full of great advice on meditation and daily practice, as well as a number of magickal operations.

To Ride a Silver Broomstick, Silver Ravenwolf: A Wiccan classic!

Triumph of the Moon, Ronald Hutton: A great look at the development of Witchcraft and Wicca in the United Kingdom

When, Why ..If, Robin Wood: This small tome explains ethics in magick, healing, and spell casting.